ADVANCE PRAISE FOR *DEBT FREE FOR LIFE*

"David Bach has changed the lives and taught millions to be smarter with their money and live a truly rich life through his 10 national bestselling books and regular appearances on NBC's *Today* show and the *Oprah* show. He has now taken his honest, simple, 'take action' advice to inspire and teach America to shed its debt with his latest book, *Debt Free For Life*. David has created the ultimate debt guide with the latest and greatest systems and tools to achieve financial freedom once and for all. *Debt Free For Life* is about gaining back ownership of your life and creating a brighter, financially secure future."

—Susan C. Keating, President and CEO of the
National Foundation for Credit Counseling

"David Bach understands the struggle of millions of Americans who are drowning in debt and has written the must-read of the decade to inspire and guide America to shed its debt—FOR GOOD! *Debt Free For Life* provides actionable advice and SOLUTIONS—what you can do TODAY to fix your finances and fix your debt. Bach's plan includes an abundance of tools to lead to a debt-free world of true financial security. Pick up your copy of *Debt Free For Life* today and join David's mission to turn back the tide of debt and buy back our futures—futures free from debt."

—David C. Jones, President of the Association of
Independent Consumer Credit Counseling Agencies

PRAISE FOR *THE AUTOMATIC MILLIONAIRE*

"*The Automatic Millionaire* is an automatic winner. David Bach really cares about you: on every page you can hear him cheering you on to financial fitness. No matter who you are or what your income is, you can benefit from this easy-to-apply program. Do it now. You and your loved ones deserve big bucks!"   —Ken Blanchard, coauthor of *The One Minute Manager*®

"*The Automatic Millionaire* gives you, step by step, everything you need to secure your financial future. When you do it David Bach's way, failure is not an option."   —Jean Chatzky, Financial Editor, NBC's *Today*

"David Bach's no spin financial advice is beautiful because it's so simple. If becoming self-sufficient is important to you, then this book is a must."
—Bill O'Reilly, anchor, Fox News, and author of
The O'Reilly Factor and *The No Spin Zone*

PRAISE FOR *START LATE, FINISH RICH*

"Financial wizard David Bach's new book, *Start Late, Finish Rich*, offers solid advice for getting our finances in order, no matter how old we are."
—AARP

"With feel-good sensibilities, David Bach delivers levelheaded strategies for reaching financial goals. . . . Bach's clever approach will make readers feel as if they're having a one-on-one conversation with a friendly personal financial counselor. . . . Powerful, poignant and pleasing, *Start Late, Finish Rich* can't be read fast enough."   —*Bookpage*

PRAISE FOR *SMART COUPLES FINISH RICH*

"*Smart Couples Finish Rich* teaches women and men to work together as a team when it comes to money. Bach's nine steps are powerful, yet easy to understand and fun to implement. The entire family can benefit from this great book."   —Robert T. Kiyosaki, author of *Rich Dad, Poor Dad*

"I know how hard it is to make a personal-finance book user-friendly. Bach has done it. *Smart Couples Finish Rich* picks up where *Smart Women Finish Rich* left off. . . . This is an easy, lively read filled with tips that made me smile and at least once made me laugh."   —*USA Weekend*

"David Bach offers a prescription both to avoid money conflicts and to plan a harmonious future together. . . . The bottom line is action, and Bach's chatty writing style helps motivate you to that end."   —*BusinessWeek*

PRAISE FOR *SMART WOMEN FINISH RICH*

"Inspires women to start planning today for a secure financial future. Every woman can benefit from this book. . . . Bach is an excellent money coach."
—John Gray, bestselling author of
Men Are from Mars, Women Are from Venus

"David Bach is the one expert to listen to when you're intimidated by your finances. His easy-to-understand program will show you how to afford your dreams."
—Anthony Robbins, author of *Awaken the Giant Within*
and *Unlimited Power*

"[David] Bach gets across some complicated stuff: how to organize a portfolio, keep the taxman at bay, invest in yourself, and earn more, all of which makes this book one of the best overall."   —*Working Woman*

PRAISE FOR *THE AUTOMATIC MILLIONAIRE HOMEOWNER*

"[Bach's] cheery, can-do message . . . cuts through the intimidating challenge of buying a house for the first-timer . . . for a newcomer, it's fundamental reading."   —*USA Today*

"If you read only one real estate book this year, it should be *The Automatic Millionaire Homeowner* . . . This is one of the few real estate books that cannot be recommended too highly for both beginners and experienced homeowners."   —Robert J. Bruss, *Miami Herald*

PRAISE FOR *GO GREEN, LIVE RICH*

"Great news: there is no green premium! By demonstrating how going green can fit any budget, David Bach shows that good environmental and financial decisions go hand-in-hand. *Go Green, Live Rich* gives great tips, useful to everyone, about how to save money and the planet at once."
—Robert F. Kennedy Jr.

"*Go Green, Live Rich* is as much about saving money as it is about preserving our world of natural wonders for future generations. This is the rich-green-book of a promising tomorrow."
—Matthew Modine, Founder: Bicycle for a Day

DEBT FREE
FOR LIFE

ALSO BY DAVID BACH

Smart Women Finish Rich

Smart Couples Finish Rich

The Finish Rich Workbook

The Finish Rich Dictionary

The Automatic Millionaire

The Automatic Millionaire Workbook

Start Late, Finish Rich

The Automatic Millionaire Homeowner

Go Green, Live Rich

Fight For Your Money

Start Over, Finish Rich

DEBT FREE FOR LIFE

The Finish Rich Plan for Financial Freedom

DAVID BACH

CROWN
BUSINESS

NEW YORK

Copyright © 2010 by David Bach

All rights reserved.
Published in the United States by Crown Business, an imprint of the Crown Publishing Group, a division of Random House, Inc., New York.
www.crownpublishing.com

Crown Business is a registered trademark and the Crown Business colophon is a trademark of Random House, Inc.

The Automatic Millionaire Homeowner, The Automatic Millionaire, The Latte Factor, Smart Women Finish Rich, Smart Couples Finish Rich, and DOLP are registered trademarks of FinishRich Media, LLC.

Crown Business books are available at special discounts for bulk purchases for sales promotions or corporate use. Special editions, including personalized covers, excerpts of existing books, or books with corporate logos, can be created in large quantities for special needs. For more information, contact Premium Sales at (212) 572-2232 or e-mail specialmarkets@randomhouse.com.

Library of Congress Cataloging-in-Publication Data
Bach, David.
Debt free for life : the finish rich plan for financial freedom / David Bach.
p. cm.
1. Finance, Personal. 2. Consumer credit. I. Title.
HG179.B23425 2010
332.024'02—dc22
2010041882

ISBN 978-0-7679-2986-8
eISBN 978-0-307-59117-3

Printed in the United States of America

Jacket photograph: Deborah Feingold

10 9 8 7 6 5 4 3 2 1

First Edition

To Alatia, Jack, and James, thank you for making my life so meaningful and joyful—you are my life's greatest blessings.

I love you with all my heart.

CONTENTS

ACKNOWLEDGMENTS

Truly to my readers, THANK YOU, THANK YOU, THANK YOU! It is hard sometimes for me to believe that *Debt Free For Life* is my twelfth book in the FinishRich Series—and that there are now more than seven million of the FinishRich books in print around the world. So, I want to start by first thanking YOU, my readers. As a writer you spend literally thousands of hours often on a book by yourself—and then you wait and wonder if what you wrote really makes a difference? Fortunately for me, so many of you write to me on a daily basis that I know my work is helping you, and for that I am deeply grateful. YOU inspire me to keep doing what I do. I am deeply humbled and grateful for your trust, your love, and your constant encouragement. THANK YOU sounds small, but it is truly coming from my heart, and if I could give each and every one of you a hug or high five, I would! Thousands of you have asked me to write this book, and I truly hope it meets your expectations and helps you. I take your investment of your money and, most important, your time and trust seriously, and I am again so grateful that you continue to follow me from book to book.

I am equally grateful to the many people who have worked so tirelessly with me over the years to support my message of financial hope and action. I feel incredibly fortunate to have so many dedicated colleagues who truly care about making a difference in the world. There are so many of you to thank, and what follows is only a short list, but please know if I have left you out of this acknowledgment, you are still in my heart and prayers.

I want first to start by thanking Oprah Winfrey. The opportunity to reach your millions of viewers allowed me to help millions more people than I could have ever dreamed possible. I am literally thanked weekly by readers who say, "I saw you on *Oprah,* and changed my life because of what you said on her show." I will always be grateful to you and your world-class team at Harpo for giving me the platform to teach people all over the world how to be smarter with their money. The Debt Diet Series I did with you inspired me to spend the last five years teaching America how to get out of debt and led directly to this book. To Katy Davis, Candy Carter and Dana Brooks, and your fabulous teams who helped us make all of our shows together so powerful, you are my guiding angels. Thank you for believing in me and my message.

To the team at NBC's *Today* show, I am so grateful to all of you for giving me the incredible opportunity to be a weekly contributor to your "Money 911" segments for the past two years. Getting to answer America's financial questions each week has been an amazing experience. A special thank-you to Marc Victor, Jacklyn Levin, Gil Reisfield, Amanda Avery, Katherine Buckley, Elizabeth Neumann, Donna Nicholls, and Michele Leone for your production expertise and the hard work you do to make these segments as fantastic as they are. A big thank-you to Matt Lauer, Meredith Vieira, Ann Curry, and Natalie Morales for being so wonderful to work with. And a special hug to Al Roker—you make each week a blast! And to Jean Chatzky, Sharon Epperson, and Carmen Ulrich Wong—you are world-class experts who make each show fantastic.

To Allan Mayer, we've worked together now for well over a decade. Words can't express how grateful I am for our incredible working relationship. Your feedback is invaluable and you make me better each time you edit my books. Thank you so much for making this, our ninth book together, go so smoothly. To Zac Bissonette and Helen Huntley, thank you for your contributions to this book.

To Stephen Breimer, thank you once again for your unceasing efforts to protect and promote my brand and business. Every day I thank my lucky stars that you represent me. Kudos to you, my friend—I salute you!

To my new partners at Equifax and the DebtWise.com team, I can't wait to spread our message about the "Debt Free Challenge." We have set a huge goal for ourselves to inspire a million people to get out of debt in 2011—and I am looking forward to the journey! To BKV and Jackson Spalding, your work is truly outstanding. Here's to a very successful and fun launch.

To my team at Random House, this is our eleventh book together! I am incredibly grateful that I have been in business with the same publisher my entire career. I deeply appreciate your commitment to me as an author. You have worked tirelessly to make my books the best of their kind in the industry. A special thanks to my new publisher Tina Constable, editor Roger Scholl, marketing director Meredith McGinnis, and publicist Tara Gilbride. To Chris Fortunato, for his tireless efforts to crash-complete the book packaging, you always rise to the occasion—thank you. To David Drake, head of publicity—you rock, sir! You are the best in the business, and I am grateful to have been working with you since 1997. Thank you, thank you—really, thank you!

To my right hands at FinishRich Media, Molly and Brittney—ladies, you are simply the best. Thank you for everything you do to keep me on schedule, pumped up, and running fast. You make doing what I do a joy!

To my parents, Bobbi and Marty, I love you both so much. Thank you for always believing in me and encouraging me. I am blessed to have parents who love me so much. To my grandma, Rose Goldsmith, you are the most dear grandmother anyone could ever ask for. To my little sister, Emily Bach, a special big hug to you. I love you so much.

To my sons, Jack and James, my little boys who soon will not be so little—your daddy loves you more than the sun, the moon, and the stars. You boys are my greatest joy. To Alatia Bradley, my sweetheart, soul mate, and best friend—thank you for making every day and everything better. I truly feel each and every day grateful that you came into my life. I love you!

To my EO buddies, David Rich, Roark Dunn, Brian Martin, Jay Kubasssek, Chris Power, Andrew Christodoulides, Navid Moradi, Mitch Schamroth, Laurence Levi, you guys have been my business soul mates. Thank you for your friendship and constant encouragement!

And again, lastly to you, my readers. I could fill this page with "thank you"s and it wouldn't begin to express how deeply grateful and blessed I feel to be able to do what I do for you. You made it all possible. I am humbled by your faith and trust in me—and thankful for how many of you regularly take the time to email me your success stories. I can't reply to every email I get, but I do read them all, and I am truly grateful on a daily basis for your words of encouragement and your good wishes! I thank you from the bottom of my heart.

David Bach
New York
September 2010

INTRODUCTION

GOODBYE, DEBT—HELLO, FREEDOM!

Early in the winter of 2010, I was sitting in the greenroom preparing to go on the NBC's *Today* show to do our weekly "Money 911" segment. The segment had been airing for more than two years. Each week we would take questions from viewers about their money. This week, most of the questions seemed to be about debt. Reading over the questions, it hit me—in just two years, we had gone from being asked mainly about investments to being asked almost entirely about personal debt.

As I thought about this, a friend in the greenroom interrupted me with a question of her own. "David," she asked, "what's your take on '*good debt*' vs. '*bad debt*'?"

Almost automatically, I started giving her the standard answer about how good debts are generally considered to be debts you incur to buy things that can go up in value—like a home or a college education—while bad debts are things like credit card balances, where you've borrowed money to buy things that will depreciate or go down in value, like most consumer goods. But then I stopped in mid-answer and looked at her.

"You know something?" I said. "The truth is that this recession has changed everything. Homes are going down in value and people with college degrees are looking for jobs. Forget what I was just telling you. Forget about the idea of 'good debt' and 'bad debt.' The truth is that when you're in debt, it doesn't matter what you've borrowed the money for. The only thing that matters is whether or not you can afford to pay it back. And if you can't, *all* debt is bad debt."

My friend smiled sadly. "Tell me about it," she said. "My home is underwater, and my mortgage rate is going up and I can't refinance because my credit score has dropped." She shook her head and sighed.

"So what do I do? *What's your advice to people like me?*"

THE BEST INVESTMENT YOU CAN MAKE NOW

This time I stopped and thought before answering. "Here's what I think," I finally said, "and this is what I'm going to be telling everyone now. **The best investment you can make over the next five years is going to be paying off your debts. So my advice is to pay off what you owe as fast as you can.** The faster you pay off your debt, the faster you will achieve financial freedom."

I went on to tell my friend that at Morgan Stanley, where I had worked as a financial advisor for nearly a decade, the clients of ours who focused on paying off their debt were able to retire an average of ten years earlier than those who didn't.

"So does this mean I should stop putting money into my 401(k) plan and instead use it to pay off my mortgage?" she asked.

I shook my head. "Of course not," I replied. "You should never stop 'paying yourself first.' What you need to do is cut down your spending so you can stop going into debt, and pay off your debt faster. Trust me—getting out of debt has never been more important than it is now. Being *debt free for life* should be your new financial goal."

And with that I headed into the studio with Al Roker to

answer America's never-ending questions about managing their money and getting out of debt.

ARE YOU TIRED OF BEING IN DEBT?
DO YOU WANT A NEW WAY OUT?

If you're like most people, you're probably familiar with the idea of "good debt" and "bad debt." Millions of Americans believe in this idea. In fact, millions of Americans have based their lives on it. At the heart of this belief is the notion that good debt makes you rich and bad debt keeps you poor. You only borrow to buy assets, and you shouldn't borrow to buy things that drop in value. It makes sense; it seems logical.

I, too, used to believe it. But you know what? I no longer do. And neither should you. Why? *Because the idea that there's such a thing as good debt and bad debt is a myth.*

The truth is we've been misled.

- We've been misled by billions of dollars' worth of advertising that gets us to buy things we don't really need.

- We've been misled by a multibillion-dollar credit card industry that tells us the good life can be ours for the taking when we use their credit cards.

- We've been misled by the banks that loaned us money for homes they knew millions of us couldn't really afford.

- We've been misled by the subprime lenders who promoted the idea that we were "silly" to keep equity in our homes when we could "cash it out" to pay off our credit cards.

- We've been misled by a tax system that promotes heavy borrowing by offering tax deductions.

- We were sold a bill of goods—or, more accurately, a bill of loans (trillions of dollars of them). And now this bill has come due, and our debt has become our personal financial prison.

Are you tired of being in debt? Are you tired of waking up each morning to face an ever larger pile of bills? Like my friend in the greenroom, do you find yourself working harder than ever to pay for things you no longer care about—or even want to own?

If so, you are not alone. Millions of people feel the same way—and like you, they are ready for a life free from debt. *A life where you own your life—rather than lease it.*

The good news is that there is a way out of this nightmare. There is a better way to live—starting today—a way that will allow you to be debt free for life!

THE MIRACLE OF COMPOUND INTEREST— IN REVERSE!

Here's the truth: DEBT IS DEBT. Probably the most important lesson of the great recession we've just lived through is that there's no such thing as a good debt if you can't afford to pay it off. When you can't make the payments, the only difference between "good" debts and "bad" debts is that the bad variety can destroy your financial life much more quickly.

Now, don't get me wrong. We need to be able to borrow money. Without a lending industry and the ability to borrow, we could not function as a society. Borrowing to build assets can make sense—*if you have a real plan to repay your debt.* But if you don't have a plan, look out! Debt is all about basic math. It is the miracle of compound interest in reverse, which is to say that if you don't stay on top of it, it will mushroom faster than you can imagine—and crush you before you know what's happening.

This is one big reason why I wrote this book: to give you the plan you need to pay off your debts faster then you ever would have thought possible.

DEBT FREE FOR LIFE:
A NEW APPROACH AND A NEW ATTITUDE

It is time for us to rethink entirely the way we manage our money and our debt. If the great recession has taught us anything, it is that the less debt we have, the better off we are. With this in mind, I am now on a mission to inspire America to shed its debt. I believe it is time for us to buy back our freedom, and I know that together we can do it. This is another reason why I have written *Debt Free For Life*—and why I hope you will read it and act on its advice starting today.

Debt Free For Life is my twelfth book. It is very possible that you have read (or at least heard of) one of my previous titles. As I write this, there are more than 7 million copies of my FinishRich books in print around the world. I am known for my honest, simple, and "take action" advice about finances, and I've been privileged to inspire millions around the world to be smarter with their money and truly live a rich life. Perhaps you have seen me on television on NBC's *Today* show, "Money 911" segments, or on Oprah's "Debt Diet" series, or on CNBC's "The Millionaire Inside" series. Then again, maybe this is our first visit together—and if it is, welcome! In either case, I want to say, THANK YOU. Thank you for your time and your trust that I may have a plan for you—a plan that will make you DEBT FREE FOR LIFE!

ELIMINATE YOUR DEBT— AND BUY BACK YOUR FREEDOM!

So why did I pick this moment to write a book on getting out of debt—and why should you spend a few hours reading it? Why is it time to buy back our freedom and focus on our own personal economy?

The answer is simple:

In our new economy, getting out of debt fast is the most important financial move you and your family can make.

There are three reasons for this:

First, I believe that our debt is out of control.

Every day I get tons of questions from my readers—maybe you're one of them—and most of them are related to debt. You email me at **www.finishrich.com**, you post at my community at **www.facebook.com/davidbach**, and you call in to the various shows I do. What I hear from you is scary. You've got credit card balances you can't pay off, mortgage loans and home equity lines that are crushing you, student loans, car loans, medical debt—you name it. "David," I hear over and over again, "I'm drowning—what in the world can I do?" Or: "David, I have had enough—**I want to retire someday and**

not be worried about money—how can I get out of debt once and for all?" The fact is that we've lost control of our debt both individually and as a nation—and this has to change. We have come to a point in history where personally, nationally, and even globally the devastating effect of debt is beginning not only to crush the human spirit, but also our ability to be free and ultimately secure.

Second, I believe the world *is* waking up to the problem of debt.

National economies around the globe have been shaken to their core because of debt loads. Europe fears more economic collapses—and many experts worry that the United States itself is on the brink of bankruptcy. (I'm not there yet, but I am concerned—and you should be, too.) What I know for sure is that the debt we have the best chance of controlling is our own. There are dozens of books today about "whose fault it is." But I'm not interested in playing the blame game. We can debate who's to blame for America's trillion-dollar deficits— or we can focus on our own families' "deficits" and get our personal finances together. This book is about SOLUTIONS— what you can do to fix your situation! It's about *you—your* finances—*your* debt! The faster you are debt free, the faster you will be protected from things you can't control, like our national budget deficits.

Third, I am convinced that MILLIONS ARE READY TO TAKE ACTION.

There is a movement in this country right now to pay down debt and save money. As I write this in the summer of 2010, savings rates are up to 6%, the highest in two decades, and debt levels are falling. Millions of people, including you, are ready to be debt free. We've had enough of the burden and worry that debt creates. You are ready to take action—smart action—that will help you become financially free and secure. Many of you have written to me, sharing that you are tired of working so hard for so long—and winding up with so little. You are ready to get off of the treadmill of going to work, making money, spending money, going to work, making money, spending money. You are ready to be FREE! You are ready for new ideas and new tools that will help you become smarter about your money and your debt. You are ready to be DEBT FREE FOR LIFE!

My previous books contained great tools for debt reduction. But in this new, challenging economy, I realized I needed to create a new, updated plan with the latest and greatest systems to help you get out of debt TODAY. So welcome! Let's spend a few hours together—and get going on a new plan that will lead you to a debt-free world of true financial security. It may not be as easy to get out of debt as it was to get in, but trust me—the benefits that will come from this journey you're about to begin will be more than worth the effort.

Do you believe as I do? Do these three beliefs of mine make sense to you at a gut level? If they do, then please keep reading. Together, we can turn back this tide of debt and buy back our futures. **It is time for a better way of life—one free from debt.**

MY GIFT TO YOU

THE DEBT FREE FOR LIFE CHALLENGE VIDEO SERIES AT WWW.FINISHRICH.COM

I always love to give my readers a free gift. So if you are already feeling inspired to live a debt-free life, I want to encourage you (right now!) to go online to my website at **www. finishrich.com** and join our FinishRich Community. Register and I will send you my *Debt Free For Life Challenge* video series for free—and also give you access to an amazing array of tools we've designed to help you stay motivated to get out of debt.

Through our website, you can access "The David Bach Debt Free Challenge" site, an online community where you can interact with like-minded people committed to becoming debt free. Our goal is to inspire one million people to join us on this challenge. On the website, you'll find videos, audios, and interviews with me and other experts to help you live debt free for life. You'll also find contests you can enter to win prizes.

This book also comes with another gift: a free trial of an amazing new debt-reduction system called Debt Wise (**www.debtwise.com**) that I'll talk more about later. This revolutionary online tool will help you reduce your debt by creating a FAST-PAY PLAN to pay off your loans years early and save you thousands of dollars in interest charges. It is powered by Equifax, the nation's leading credit bureau—and as part of the package, you'll also get access to an Equifax credit score.

SHARE YOUR SUCCESS STORIES—
AND YOUR QUESTIONS

As always, I want to hear from you about how this book affected your life. This book includes real success stories from real people who have achieved the results you may be looking for. Most of these stories came directly from people who wrote to me after reading one of my books and applying what they had learned. You can find hundreds more at **www.finishrich. com**. Read them and ask yourself, "If they can do it, why not me?"

The answer is you can—and I can't wait to hear about when you do.

So if you have a success story to share, I'd love to know about it—and if you have questions I want to hear those, too. In either case, you can email me directly at **success@ finishrich.com**.

Now, are you ready to become debt free for life? Are you ready to buy back your freedom? Great—let's get started on your journey to become DEBT FREE FOR LIFE! Your new plan awaits you in the next chapter.

Live Rich,
David Bach

DEBT FREE FOR LIFE SUCCESS STORY

My wife and I read *The Automatic Millionaire* and *Start Late, Finish Rich* on vacation at the beach in 2008. These books inspired us to greatly accelerate paying off our credit cards and other debt. We used your DOLP system and within

20 months, we had paid off our credit cards and three car loans—almost $65,000 in all—while increasing my wife's 403(b) retirement plan and continuing to max out my 401(k) plan. With our new-found cash flow from not paying debt, we have also been able to double our charitable giving and we are saving to buy our own beach house, both as an investment and to enjoy for personal use. And the story gets BETTER! Our son Jeremy, who's in the military and deployed in Afghanistan, told me he read *The Automatic Millionaire* and it inspired him to quit smoking, allowing him to save $2,000 annually! From 5,000 miles away—when I was sharing with him the success we're having thanks to *The Automatic Millionaire*—he shouted, "Dad, that's the book I was telling you about!" Thank you again for motivating us and turbo-charging our way out of debt!

Joseph G.
Detroit, MI

CHAPTER ONE

WHO PUT AMERICA INTO DEBT—AND HOW YOU CAN GET YOURSELF OUT

Once upon a time (in the decades after the Great Depression), Americans desired a life of financial freedom. To our grandparents and great-grandparents, this meant staying out of debt. Living through the Great Depression, our great-grandparents learned the hard way that debt was bad, that owing money could destroy your life. So they paid for things in cash, they bought homes with big down payments, and they worked hard to pay their mortgages off as quickly as possible. They even had "mortgage-burning parties" in their backyards, where they celebrated their FREEDOM from the banks after the last payment was made. As a result, many of them were able to retire in their early sixties without financial worry. Retirement wasn't a dream for our great-grandparents (and often our grandparents, who learned prudent financial behavior from their parents), it was an American Promise! For them, the American Dream was real—you went to work, you worked hard, you saved money, you paid down your debt, and then you retired with a pension and Social Security, and you lived happily ever after.

AMERICANS CARRY $12 TRILLION IN DEBT—
WE DESERVE BETTER

These days, the American Dream of financial freedom—freedom from worry, freedom from living paycheck to paycheck—has become a nightmare. We bought the myth—or, I should say, we bought the lie and turned it into a myth. As I write this, the Federal Reserve reports that Americans are on the hook for nearly *$12 TRILLION* in consumer and mortgage debt. This translates to an average of $49,000 of debt per family; in California and Nevada, the average tops $70,000. At the beginning of 2010, roughly 54 million Americans families owed a total of $866 billion in credit card debt—or an average of just over $16,000 each.

At the same time, home equity has been dropping—by trillions of dollars over the last few years—as a result of the real estate declines, while unemployment has stayed stubbornly high. With 70% of us living paycheck to paycheck, nearly seven million Americans have fallen behind on their mortgage payments, and as the *New York Times* reported, **"An astonishing $1.3 trillion of consumer debt is delinquent, with $986 billion seriously so—90 days late and counting."** Not surprisingly, the number of personal bankruptcies has been skyrocketing, reaching nearly two million in 2010—a 100% increase in just five years.

Our government is in even worse shape, having gone from a balanced budget in fiscal 2001 to a $1.4-TRILLION deficit in fiscal 2009 (and a projected $1.2-trillion deficit for fiscal 2010). The idea that we should all spend less than we make seems to have been forgotten, as the American Dream gets stolen, one loan at time. One has to truly wonder what has happened. How did we get here? And most important, what do we really want and what will we do about it?

HOW IS YOUR DEBT DOING?

So let's be honest. Do you have more debt than you want?

Chances are, you do—or you wouldn't have picked up this book.

Are you paying a huge percentage of your paycheck each month to just cover the interest or make the minimum payments on what you've borrowed for your home, your car, your student loans, your credit cards, etc.? Are you frustrated that no matter how hard you try to pay off your debt, it seems to take forever and you don't see any progress happening fast enough? Are you worried about your ability to retire someday because of your debt?

Or is it even worse than that? Are you unable to even make the minimum payments on your loans and find yourself falling behind, with your debt growing? Did you know that if you are carrying $10,000 in credit card debt and your card is charging you 25% interest, and you're making minimum payments, it will take you *more than 22 years* to pay off your debt? Did you know that if you have a $250,000 mortgage with a low fixed rate of 6%, paying it off over 30 years would cost you just under $540,000?

MILLIONS OF AMERICANS ARE IN DEBT AND WANT OUT

The reason I am sharing these figures with you is not to be negative or depress you. What I want to do is start this book and your journey to being debt free for life with the truth. **And the truth is that MILLIONS of Americans are hugely in debt and want out!**

One credit bureau estimates that more than 45 million

people (or roughly one out of every five Americans with a credit score) want to improve their financial well-being through debt reduction. Indeed, in the recent rush to take advantage of low mortgage rates by refinancing, about a third of all loan applicants have been putting money into their homes—meaning they are reducing the amount they owe—rather than taking money out. Similarly, a record number of homeowners are switching from 30-year mortgages to 15-year mortgages in order to own their homes debt free faster.

So you see—you're not alone! And like so many others, you can do something quickly to change your situation, reduce your debt, and become DEBT FREE FOR LIFE!

THE DEBT FREE FOR LIFE PROMISE: WHY YOU SHOULD READ THIS BOOK— AND ACT ON IT!

It's easy to get into debt. Getting out is another story. Some so-called debt-settlement companies will tell you, "We can cut your debt in half in minutes and save you thousands of dollars." Sorry, but that's just nonsense!

This book is about the truth. It offers an honest plan that will work—*if you work it!* I know there are some of you who are reading this book because you are really drowning in debt and are looking for a life preserver. If this is your situation, I believe this book can be the life raft that gets you back to dry land. But let me be clear: You don't need to be in over your head to benefit from this book or the **Debt Free For Life Plan** I'm about to share. This book is about a totally new approach to building financial freedom that stresses "paying down your debt" so you can buy back your freedom. I've been teaching my readers for years how to pay down their debt. Maybe I have taught you already. But the **Debt Free For Life Plan** is a revolutionary new system that will make paying off your debt easier than it has ever been.

Most people who apply the **Debt Free For Life Plan** I will share in the pages that follow will be able to get themselves out of debt an average of 15 years faster and save themselves at least $30,000 in the process. Some of you will do this even faster than that and be out of debt in as little as seven, five, or even just three years. (I've even seen people get out of debt using these tools in less than a year.) How quickly you can do it will depend on you—on how much debt you have, how much you can cut your expenses, and how fast you want to make it happen.

Some of you have old debt that is so long overdue that you can no longer be required to pay it, and you don't even know it. (You will once you read this book.) Some of you can save six figures by simply applying one idea in this book (you'll find it on page 124 in the chapter about mortgages).

The fact is that the math of debt is not complicated. You simply need to apply the principles I will share and then, like the Nike slogan says, "Just Do It."

Now don't get me wrong—I am not promising you overnight freedom from debt. But what I can promise is that the moment you start on this plan, you will begin to feel better. Just knowing that you have a plan in place to pay down your debt in the right order, the right way—a plan you can carry out yourself that will save you thousands of dollars in interest fees and cut years off your indebtedness—will truly lighten your burden, however light or heavy it may be.

I also promise you that having less debt will feel GREAT. *Debt creates fear. Not having it creates peace of mind.* This may sound like a cliché, but it's true. When you have less debt, you will feel more FREE. You will have fewer worries, less stress, less tension, fewer fights at home. In short, your life will have less fear and more serenity. Not only that, but you will also be able to build wealth faster.

A DEBT FREE FOR LIFE SUCCESS STORY

I cannot express my gratitude for what your books *Start Late, Finish Rich* and *Smart Women Finish Rich* have done for me. They've helped me change not only my financial life, but my physical life as well. My "latte factor" (the way I wasted money) was food! I could not believe how much I was wasting on "occasional" snacks. It was atrocious—and so was my waist line! The one major thing you said that stuck in my head and changed my actions was, "Is this purchase really necessary?" I now ask myself that question every time I think about spending money—and doing this has truly changed my life. I have saved over $6,000 in six months and I have lost 21 pounds. David, you are a lifesaver, in more ways than one! Thank you for everything!

Nicole D.
Yuba City, CA

HOW THIS BOOKS WORKS:
THE FINISH RICH PLAN TO ACHIEVE
FINANCIAL FREEDOM

We're going to start the process of achieving financial freedom by learning how to change your mindset, cut your expenses, and live within your means. Next, I'll show you how the credit card companies imprison you with tricks and traps in order to keep you in debt for life. Once you understand their games, you'll be able to fight back and win—and achieve real financial freedom.

Then we will look at what I call the DEBT FREE FOR LIFE MINDSET. This will help you get to the root of why you got into debt in the first place—and how you can get out of it once and for all.

Debt is often created because, without thinking about it, we spend money we don't have to buy things we were *subconsciously PROGRAMMED* to buy. Re-read that sentence! Companies spend BILLIONS AND BILLIONS of marketing dollars each and every year to bombard you with enticements to spend money. Trust me when I tell you that just about anyone can get out of debt once they become conscious of this. On the other hand, if your mindset on debt is wrong, you'll probably never get out of debt—and if you do, the odds are that you'll get right back in. That's not good enough. We want you DEBT FREE FOR LIFE!

YOUR DO-IT-YOURSELF SYSTEM— THE DEBT FREE FOR LIFE TOOL KIT

Once we've got your DEBT FREE FOR LIFE MINDSET right, we'll look at my do-it-yourself system for getting out of debt. It's called DOLP®, which stands for "Done On Last Payment." This is a simple system that I have taught for more a decade to prioritize your debt so you can pay it off as fast and cheaply as possible. One of the great things about DOLP is that you can do it from the comfort and safety of your own home with zero technology. All you need is a pen or pencil and a sheet or two of paper.

After we cover DOLP, I will share with you the truly revolutionary new debt-reduction program I mentioned called DebtWise.com. I was so impressed with DebtWise.com when it was launched in 2009 that I reached out to the company behind it, Equifax, and partnered with them to bring it to North America and make it the best online program in the world for debt reduction. As I mentioned in the Introduction, this book includes a free trial offer for DebtWise.com, along with a free credit score from Equifax.

What makes DebtWise.com so revolutionary is that it's powered by one of the three major U.S. credit bureaus. This connection enables it to automatically access all your credit records in seconds—securely. As a result, in less than ten minutes with DebtWise.com, you will be able to create and implement a complete system to pay down your debt automatically! You will also be able to calculate your own "Debt Freedom Day"—the exact date, based on how much you owe and how aggressive a payment plan you choose, that you will truly be debt free.

WHERE TO GO FOR HELP— WHOM CAN YOU TRUST?

Although I believe that most of you who read this book should be able to implement the do-it-yourself systems I will teach you to reduce your debt, I know that some people would prefer to have the help of a professional who can personally help guide them through the process. If you're one of these people, don't worry. Once I've finished explaining the ins and outs of

DOLP and DebtWise.com, I will share everything you need to know about how to find a qualified expert who can help you get out of debt.

As part of this process, I will explain in detail how the non-profit consumer credit counseling world works and what they can do for you. We'll also explore the debt settlement industry (the "for profit" debt-reduction business) and what to watch out for, since this is a world filled with pitfalls. This is important for everyone to know, whether you plan to seek out counseling or not.

We will then cover the secrets to getting out of debt that the credit card companies don't want me to share, including how to get your interest rates lowered, your late fees waived, your annual fees credited back, and more. I will teach you how to negotiate for a better rate, and if you can't get a better deal on your current card, how to find a new one.

Along the way, I will share with you everything you need to know about your all-important credit score and credit reports. You'll learn how to protect and improve your score—which ultimately will make it easier to renegotiate your debt. And I will help you better understand your mortgage and student loans and what you can do to pay them off faster.

I will also cover bankruptcy (although I hope you never need this chapter) and share with you a ten-minute plan to put your entire financial life on Automatic Pilot (called The Automatic Millionaire System). Lastly, I will suggest ways to find some extra money you may not have realized you have—money you could use to help you pay down your debt.

It's a lot to cover, but I have done my best to make it all easy to understand and—most important—to ACT ON.

As in many of my previous books, each chapter ends with a series of action steps—in this case, "Debt Free For Life Action

Steps"—a condensed "to-do" list designed to remind you what you need to do and to help you keep track of your progress.

DEBT FREE FOR LIFE SUCCESS STORY

After reading *The Automatic Millionaire*, my first goal was to become debt-free within a year. So we started putting 20% of our family income toward paying off our debt. This limited our available money, but it was not a burden to us since we had decided to simplify our lives. We did this by cutting down on shopping, doing more meaningful activities, and driving our paid-off car longer instead of getting a new one with a consumer loan. Now, after only one year, we paid off all of our debt ($12,000), plus I was able to establish a four-month financial cushion for security. Before I read your book and worked your plan, I would have spent the "extra money" I was earning from freelancing on all kinds of things, but now I am determined to act differently. This time I have goals. It has not been as hard as I expected. For the first time, our family doesn't have to live paycheck to paycheck. I can't wait to achieve the next goals on my list and to put more of your advice to work. Once again thank you very much!

Brigitte R.
Seattle, WA

THANK YOU FOR TRUSTING
THAT I HAVE A PLAN FOR YOU!

Before we get started, let me once again say, THANK YOU! Many of you know me for my *New York Times* #1 bestsellers

The Automatic Millionaire and *Start Late, Finish Rich*. Others of you may know me from my bestsellers *Smart Women Finish Rich, Smart Couples Finish Rich,* or last year's bestseller *Start Over, Finish Rich.* If you liked those books, I think you will LOVE this one. Many of you have written to me over the past few years and asked me to write a book like this. I hope it meets your expectations.

But whether you've read all my previous books or this is the first book of mine that you have picked up, I am truly grateful that we are getting to spend this time together, and I'm excited to have the chance to really help you deal with your debt. Together, I truly believe we can tackle the debt that is holding us back, and move each and every one of our lives forward powerfully.

DEBT FREE FOR LIFE ACTION STEPS

Reviewing what we discussed in this chapter, here is what you should be doing right now to become Debt Free For Life. Check off each step as you accomplish it.

❏ Recognize that both as a nation and individually we have let debt get out of control—and that as a result, we are in danger of losing once and for all the American dream of financial freedom.

❏ Commit to taking action now to change your situation, reduce your debt, and become DEBT FREE FOR LIFE! Join the **"Debt Free Challenge"** at **www.finishrich.com**.

CHAPTER TWO

DEBT MATH:
HOW LENDERS KEEP YOU BROKE

Are you ready to learn more? Great—let's keep going. What I'm going to show you now is how the debt companies imprison you with basic math in order to keep you in debt for life. By learning their games, you'll be able to fight back and win—and achieve real financial freedom.

HOW TO GO BROKE ONE LOAN AT A TIME

What's amazing about debt is how easy it is to get into—and how hard it is to get out of if you don't understand the basic math. It's this math, which the debt companies understand—and we don't—that makes them rich and keeps us poor.

Let's just start with the basic math of credit card debt.

- Let's say you borrow $5,000 on one of your credit cards.

- You get your bill; it says your interest rate is 29% and your minimum payment is $175.

- You make the minimum payments—and it takes you nearly *23 years* to get out of debt.

- And it costs you $10,505.89 in interest payments.

Wow—is that really true? *How can it be?* I have posed this same question in my books for well over a decade now. How can credit card companies legally get away with not explaining this to their customers? It just doesn't seem right. You can go to a retailer and get a credit card in less than five minutes, not know the math, and as a result wind up in debt for the rest of your life.

And this basic math assumes you never pay your bills late, never go over your credit limit, or pay any annual fees. If you do any of these things, it could take you years longer to get rid of that credit card debt. **And that's just with one credit card!**

The new *Credit Card Accountability Responsibility and Disclosure Act of 2009* (otherwise known as the Credit CARD Act) is finally forcing the credit card companies to show us the truth about what I call the minimum-payment scam. It requires credit card companies to highlight on your monthly statement the insanity of the minimum-payment math—specifically, how long it will take you to pay off your current balance and how much it will cost you if you make only minimum payments. Don't take my word for this—go look at your most recent credit card statement right now. The information should be there. (And complain to the Federal Trade Commission; if this information is not spelled out on your monthly statement, your credit card company is breaking the law.)

HERE'S WHAT HAPPENS IF YOU ADD $10 A DAY

What I am about to show you will not be on your credit card statement. It should be, but it won't. Let's take another look at the payment scenario I laid out above—but this time let's make one small change.

- You borrow $5,000 on one of your credit cards.

- You decide you don't want to spend more than 23 years paying this card off—you want to be out of debt sooner.

- **So you resolve that on top of the minimum payment, you will add $10 a day to pay down this debt.**

- If you do this, you would pay off this debt in—try this on for size—*45 months!*

- Your interest charges would total just $3,203.99 (vs. $10,505.89).

- **In other words, you could save more than $7,300 with this one simple tip.**

Honestly, isn't this math pretty stunning? I mean, really? How is it possible that it took decades for the government to start forcing the credit card companies to explain this to their customers—i.e., us. The reason is simple. Ignorance is profitable—just not for you. And by the way, if the interest rate on the example above wasn't an outrageous 29% (which is what millions of Americans are now being forced to pay) and instead was the national average (which, as I write this, is 14%), using this tip would get you out of debt in just 33 months.

NOW LET'S LOOK AT MORTGAGES

Here's the basic math for mortgage debt.

- You borrow $200,000 to buy a home.

- You get a 30-year fixed mortgage at 6% annual interest.

- Your monthly mortgage payment will be $1,199.10.

- The total cost of the mortgage over the 30-year life of the loan will be $431,676.38.

- **And the interest costs will be $231,676.38!**

This mortgage math should be more familiar to you because the banks have long had to provide you with a mortgage amortization schedule when you sign your loan documents.

What they don't usually do is show you alternative payment plans. Let's look at what would happen if you added $10 a day toward your mortgage payment.

HERE'S WHAT HAPPENS IF YOU ADD $10 A DAY

- You borrow $200,000 to buy a home.

- You decide you really don't want to spend three decades paying off your mortgage—you want to be out of debt sooner.

- **So you resolve to add $10 a day to your mortgage payment.**

- If you do this, you would pay off your mortgage in a little over 18 years!

- The total cost of your mortgage would be $330,570.58 (vs. $431,676.38).

- **In other words, you would save more than $101,000 with this one simple tip.**

I just gave you two incredibly simple examples of the basic arithmetic of debt. Simply by suggesting that you add $10 a day to your minimum required payment, I shaved nearly 40 years off of what it would take to get rid of a $5,000 credit card debt. With an identical suggestion of an extra $10 a day on your mortgage payment, I cut the time it would take to pay off a 30-year mortgage almost in half. Two tips that will only cost you $20 a day—less than most families spend for a meal at McDonald's.

Later on in this book, I will give you all kinds of tools to figure out breaks like these for yourself. But for now just let it settle in how much faster you can get out of debt by making small extra payments—in the correct way.

DEBT FREE FOR LIFE SUCCESS STORY

I am a single 32-year-old mom with an 11-year-old son. I read *Smart Women Finish Rich* a few years ago and got inspired to start taking control of my spending. I had a credit card for every store in the mall, karate tuition for my son, along with medical bills piling up. After I really applied your DOLP system, I really started to feel good. Since seeing you speak in NYC in 2006, I got motivated to start paying down my debt, and writing out my financial goals. Using your tools, I have managed to pay down $45,000 in credit card debt, paid off my son's karate tuition, and even saved for a down payment for a home. I just closed on my first condo this August, and cannot begin to tell you how excited I feel. Thank you for your inspiration and guidance you provide.

Joann G.
Hartford, CT

I COULD GO ON AND ON WITH THE MATH

By now, I'm sure you are getting the point. If these two examples left you thinking, "This is just nuts—if adding $10 a day to my minimum payments can get rid of a $5,000 credit card debt in a little over a year and cut ten years off my home mortgage, I'm doing this!"—then congratulations! This tip alone will not only save you a fortune—it may also make it possible for you to retire a decade earlier (regardless of what the stock market or the economy is doing).

Now here's the great news. This book is going to do a lot more than just show you how adding $10 a day to your payments can make you debt free. This book is going to give you an entire system to prioritize your debts so you can pay them off faster and more efficiently than you probably think is possible. You're going to learn the tricks the debt industry doesn't want you to know.

The fact is that becoming debt free for life can be done, and in fact is being done. Throughout the book I'll offer a selection of remarkable stories of real people who used my Debt Free For Life Plan to get out of debt. If they can do it, you can do it. This book will be your road map—your tool kit for a life of financial freedom. *All you need to do is decide to get started.*

Are you getting excited? Good—then let's keep going. Your new plan—your new Debt Free For Life—awaits you.

A BONUS GIFT: The Latte Factor iPhone App

I know there will be some of you who may read this and think $10 a day is still a lot of money. I know it is—but I also know that most of you who are reading this can afford that and much more. The problem is that you're spending it on small things. For nearly two decades now, I have been talking about what I call the Latte Factor®. It's a phrase I coined to describe how wasting money on small things can have a huge impact on your finances, and it has gone around the world inspiring people to take charge of their financial lives. You can learn more about this online at **www.finishrich. com**. There are hundreds of Latte Factor Success Stories as well as a FREE Latte Factor iPhone app and calculator.

I hope this chapter has motivated you to stop falling for the minimum-payment scam. In fact, I truly hope that this month you do more than add $10 a day to your minimum payment, but ideally triple or quadruple it!

With that, let's take a look at your Debt Free For Life Mindset. Once we've got your thinking clear, we can get started on your action plan!

DEBT FREE FOR LIFE ACTION STEPS

❏ Pull out your most recent credit card statements and see how much it will cost you if you keep making minimum payments.

❏ Go to **www.finishrich.com** and see what would happen if you doubled the minimum payment on every one of your credit card balances.

❏ Understand the minimum-payment scam and resolve to stop falling for it.

CHAPTER THREE

THE DEBT FREE FOR LIFE MINDSET

You're ready to begin getting out of debt, aren't you? I'm sure you're motivated, and that's great—but motivation can wear off. If you want your motivation to stick, you need to be really clear about why you want to be out of debt. So our first goal is to make sure you truly understand why you want to be DEBT FREE FOR LIFE.

You may think the answer is obvious. But it's generally not what you think it is, and unless you really figure it out, you're not going to be able to get yourself out of debt for good.

How do you figure it out? By answering just seven questions—what I call the "DEBT FREE FOR LIFE QUESTIONS"—you can see whether or not you're really ready to make this journey.

WHY DO YOU REALLY WANT TO BE DEBT FREE FOR LIFE?

Before we start with the questions, let me share a little story. A few years ago, I was doing a series of shows with Oprah Winfrey called the "Debt Diet" series. What we were doing on these shows was creating a debt-reduction plan that millions of people could follow. And in fact millions of viewers who watched the shows took advantage of the online tools we created on Oprah.com and went on our Debt Diet.

After each show, we would have lunch with people selected from the audience to discuss their debt issues and what their challenges were. We wanted to better understand exactly what kind of help they needed, what they were learning, and what was working or not working for them.

At the end of one of these lunches, one of the couples we had picked came up to me. Both the husband and wife had broad grins on their faces. "We get it!" the wife announced happily.

I wasn't sure what she was talking about. "You get what?" I asked.

"We get why we really want to be out of debt," she explained. "At first, we were so focused on the details—the size of our payments, which credit card bill to pay first, that sort of thing. But then at lunch you asked us why we really want to be out of debt. We didn't have an answer—but now we do. We just decided. We both really want to be out of debt because we basically hate what we do for a living. Our daughter is disabled, and we want to be teachers who help kids like her—and if we get debt free, we can go for our dreams of teaching disabled kids. The thing is, it won't be enough for us to just pay down our credit cards. We will need to radically cut down our overhead and move to a less-expensive community. But if we do that—and we know we can with your plan—then we can really go live our dreams. We think we can do this in less than three years!"

Her husband broke in at this point. "This morning before the show we were discouraged about our debt and now we are totally excited!" he said. "This isn't really about our credit card debt—it's about what we really want our lives to be like. You helped us figure that out, David—and we're starting today. As soon as we get home. So thank you. You really did it for us."

I was thrilled for them. "Just remember," I said, "all I did was ask you the question. You found the answer. Good luck!"

And off they went to a new and more exciting life.

SEVEN BIG (BUT SIMPLE) QUESTIONS

So now let's go back to you. Imagine you are with me back-stage at Oprah's studio, like that couple. Or imagine you're at the beach with me right now (yes, I'm writing this at the beach in Del Mar, California—it's gorgeous, wish you were here).

I'm going to ask you seven simple questions about your debt. Don't get nervous. There are no RIGHT answers—only honest answers.

By the way, if you are married or in a committed long-term relationship where you share finances, you should discuss these questions with your partner. Don't assume that just because you love each other, you and your Significant Other share the same views on spending and debt. The number-one cause of divorce in this country isn't sex or religion or problems with the in-laws. It's disagreements over money, and more often than you might think, those disagreements come as a total surprise to one or both parties. Having advised thousands of couples over the years, I can tell you from first-hand experience that working on your money together significantly improves the chances not only of your succeeding financially but of your staying together happily as a couple. So make this a joint effort.

Okay? Here goes.

- Why do you want to get out of debt—or be DEBT FREE FOR LIFE?

- Why are you in debt?

- How much debt do you have?

- What percentage of your income goes to pay interest charges on your debt?

- Who would you need to help you?

- What is the worst thing that could happen if you don't get out of debt?

- When will you start?

Easy questions, right? Now let's answer them—as honestly as you can.

QUESTION ONE:
WHY DO YOU WANT TO BE DEBT FREE FOR LIFE?

I want to be debt free for life because ...

Let's look at your answer. Does it feel honest to you? Does it feel really meaningful? Does it excite you? Can you taste or feel the outcome? Is it vivid—or does it need more details?

I'll give you an example. You could write, "I'm carrying $10,000 in credit card debt, and it stresses me out, and I'm worried every month when the bills come. I'm paying 29% in annual interest, and I feel stupid wasting this money. Because of it there are so many other things I can't afford to do. So the faster I pay it down, the better. I know when I pay it off I will feel GREAT."

That was a simple example, but you get the gist.

Then again, your answer could be much more vivid and deeper. You might read that question and come up with a deeply personal spiritual reason. I remember when I asked this question at a seminar I once gave, a reader named Richard choked up and nearly burst into tears. "My entire life I have been afraid of being homeless, being left in the street with nothing," he said. "My father was an alcoholic who walked out on us when I was six. My mom and I and my brother and sister were left penniless. We ended up on the streets, living with crack addicts, then homeless shelters. For years, we went to bed hungry. I never felt safe. The kids at school made fun of me because of my beat-up clothes and because I smelled. I'm afraid every day that this could happen again."

Richard paused for a moment, then continued. "I want to know that I will never be homeless again. That my savings will always be safe, and that I won't need to depend on anyone. I also want my two kids to always be safe from financial worry and I would like to help them someday buy a home. The sooner I pay down my mortgage, the sooner I feel like I can focus on building up a trust to help them someday buy their own homes. Helping my kids own a home feels like the greatest gift I could give them other than my unconditional love. Knowing I am working toward these goals will give me peace of mind, and achieving them I believe will bring me serenity. I feel better just imagining it happen right now."

So again, I ask you:

Why do you want to be DEBT FREE FOR LIFE?

Write your answer in the space provided earlier or on a piece of paper or in your journal, if you have one (I hope you do). If you're married or in a relationship, do this exercise with your partner. This journey toward becoming Debt Free For Life is a really great one to go on together.

Having this conversation with yourself and the ones you love can help you go from being fearful to being hopeful. (And don't worry if right now you don't know how you will get there. That part will come later.)

> **QUESTION TWO:**
> **WHY ARE YOU IN DEBT?**

My goal with this question is not to have you beat yourself up, but rather to have you face the truth about how you got where you are today. Did something tragic happen, like a medical problem? Did you lose a job? Did you buy a bigger house than you could afford? Did you live beyond your means?

What really happened? You may not be living paycheck to paycheck, but are simply carrying more debt than you are comfortable with. How did you get there?

Just answer the question from your heart as honestly as you can.

I got into the amount of debt I have today because ...

QUESTION THREE:
HOW MUCH DEBT DO YOU HAVE?

In the next chapter, we will cover exactly how to determine how much debt you have, and I'll provide you with worksheets to help you do this. For now, just make an educated guess. How much debt do you have that you want to pay off? Go ahead and write it down now.

I estimate that my total debt (house, cars, student loans, credit cards—you name it) as of [insert today's date] _____ is $_____.

QUESTION FOUR:
WHAT PERCENTAGE OF YOUR INCOME GOES TO PAY INTEREST CHARGES ON YOUR DEBT?

This is probably not a question you can answer right now. More than likely, you'll need to come back to this one after you read the next chapter. But it may be the most eye-opening question of the eight. What I want you to do is pull out your mortgage statement, your car loan statement, your student loan statement, your credit card statement—the most recent statement for every loan you have—and figure out exactly how much of your monthly payment goes to interest charges. For example, say your mortgage payment is $2,000 a month. Chances are that less than $150 of that goes toward paying down the principal. The rest is going to interest. The same is true for your credit card bill. If you make a minimum payment of $200 a month on a credit card bill, most likely all but maybe $20 of that is eaten up by interest charges. In order to know where you really stand, you need to break out how much of your debt payments go to interest and how much to principal. This may involve calling your lenders and asking them to give you the facts. And the answers may shock you. Once you add up all the interest you are paying, you may find that more than half your take-home pay is going right into the lenders' pockets— without helping you make one inch of financial progress. Remember, the only time you get ahead with debt is when you pay down principal. This is why so many people (maybe you're one of them) complain about paying so much on their loans— and never seeing the balances shrink. Frustrating, right? It's why you need to know what proportion of your take-home pay is going toward paying interest charges.

My *total interest payments*
each month are: $_____
My take-home pay each
month is: $_____
The proportion of my take-home
pay that goes to pay interest
charges is: _____%
(divide your interest payments by your
take-home pay to get answer above)

QUESTION FIVE:
WHO CAN HELP YOU GET OUT OF DEBT?

Now I want you to think about whom you may need to turn to in order to help you get out of debt. This book is designed for you to be able to do it yourself—meaning that if you follow the plan I lay out and use the tools I provide (either my DOLP® system or the Debt Wise tool I created with Equifax), you should be able to get yourself out of debt. That said, maybe you're not the do-it-yourself type. Maybe you feel you'll need a professional credit counselor to help guide you through the process. If that's true for you, then great—write it down. And even if doing it yourself is not a problem for you, if you have a family, you are going to need their help and support to get out of debt. Trust me—it's really hard to get out of debt if the people around you are spending you back into it. So if you have a spouse and/or kids, you may want to add them to your answer here. Also, you should definitely add me to your list—because I am committed to helping you. (Along those lines, aside from reading this book, the first thing you can do toward letting me help you is to join our community and get my DEBT FREE FOR LIFE VIDEO SERIES, which is free for you at **www.finishrich.com.**)

I have decided that the following people will help me to get out of debt:

QUESTION SIX:
WHAT'S THE WORST THING THAT COULD HAPPEN
IF YOU DON'T GET OUT OF DEBT?

I include this question because it's important that you face your fear about debt. Being in debt is an everyday thing. Debt is always with you. You have it right now. So my question to you is really simple: What will your life look like in the future if you *don't* deal with your debt?

Facing your fear about your debt is not being pessimistic—it's being honest. And the more honest you are right now, the better. So tell yourself the truth. Write down what your worst-case scenario could be.

In fact, once you write out your worst fear, you will more than likely realize it isn't going to happen—and just realizing that will make you feel better. And if you really believe the worst could happen, then writing it out will motivate you even more to act quickly and decisively to start dealing with your debt.

The worst thing that could happen if I don't deal with my debt is ...

QUESTION SEVEN:
WHEN WILL YOU START?

On the next page, you will find the "Debt Free For Life Pledge," which I've created to mark your new commitment to leading a debt-free life. By signing it, you are making a promise not to me but to yourself and your loved ones—a promise that you are truly headed toward a new life of financial freedom. I hope you will consider that reading this book means you have already started the process of becoming debt free for life. If you do, you should sign the pledge and put down today's date. It will be nice when you celebrate your Debt Freedom Day to pull this paper out and see in your own handwriting the promise you made on the day you started to change your life.

NOW TAKE AND SIGN THE
DEBT FREE FOR LIFE PLEDGE

I _____[insert your name] commit to be out of debt by _____ [insert date].

I believe that paying down my debt and being DEBT FREE FOR LIFE is critically important, and I am ready to work to make it happen.

I will start my journey to being out of debt on _____ (insert date).

Signed _____

DEBT FREE FOR LIFE SUCCESS STORY

In August of 2007, I read an article you wrote on Yahoo Finance about your DOLP method of paying off your credit cards. At the time, I had $46,000 in credit card debt and didn't believe I could ever get out from under it. Now it's August of 2010 and we are down to two credit cards and our debt is down to $12,000! One of those cards will be paid off in a matter of months, and I expect to be completely debt free by next year. I can finally see the light at the end of the tunnel. Not only that, but we are living within our means and have some savings (no small feat these days). Thank you for your rational and systematic approach. You have made a real difference in our lives.

Phil L.
Santa Cruz, CA

TAKE THE PLEDGE AND WIN

Now go to **www.finishrich.com** or **www.facebook.com/davidbach** and take the "Debt Free Pledge" online. Show publicly that you are ready to be Debt Free for LIFE! And share this with your friends and loved ones. Let's start a movement together!

You can also join our Debt Free Challenge and win online goodies for signing up and earn prizes as you stay on your plan. All details are on the Debt Free Life Challenge website, which you will find at **www.finishrich.com**.

THINKING IS OFTEN THE HARDEST THING TO DO— AND YOU JUST DID IT!

Congratulations on taking the time to read my questions and answer them. Even if you haven't stopped reading and started writing, the fact that you asked the questions of yourself means you have started the process. And if you *have* taken the time to write the answers (as I hope you did—or will do), then well done! I'm proud of you. Now let's get started on my do-it-yourself system for getting out of debt. As I said earlier, all you need is a pen or pencil, a sheet or two of paper—and the desire to be Debt Free For Life.

DEBT FREE FOR LIFE ACTION STEPS

❏ Ask yourself the seven Debt Free For Life Mindset questions—and answer them as honestly as you can.
❏ Take and sign the Debt Free For Life pledge at **www. finishrich.com**.
❏ Go online and share your pledge publicly.

CHAPTER FOUR

IF YOU'RE IN A HOLE,
STOP DIGGING

You just answered the seven questions about why you want to be out of debt—and you've got your Debt Free For Life Mindset started! Well done. Now before we jump into the "how to crush your debt" portion of this book, I want to mention one absolutely vital idea you need to understand and accept if you are going to have any chance of becoming debt free for life. It's the kind of thing that you might think goes without saying, and to be honest I debated with myself about whether or not to include it here. In the end, I figured it couldn't hurt. So here goes.

A big part of getting out of debt is realizing that when you are in a hole, you have to stop digging. This is one of the great truths of achieving financial freedom: you can't become debt free if you keep piling on the debt. Too often I meet people who do a great job of paying down one credit card, only to start piling up debt on a new credit card the moment they get a "special offer" in the mail. Or I meet someone who tells me that they've just paid off their car—and then six months later, they are driving a brand-new car with a new lease payment! Or they get close to paying off their mortgage, and then they refinance, lowering their payments but stretching out the term of their debt. Hello! The point here is to get your debt paid off for good!

HOW MY CREDIT CARDS
WOUND UP IN THE MICROWAVE

When I share the idea that when you are in a debt hole you need to stop digging, I'm speaking from experience. You see, back when I was in college, I had huge problems with spending in general and credit cards in particular. By the beginning of my senior year, I owed more than ten thousand dollars in credit card debt. I had three cards and was desperate to get them paid off, but nothing seemed to work for me. I tried everything—all the stupid tricks—even the dumb one where you put your credit cards in a bowl of water and freeze them, so if you're tempted to use them, you have to wait for the ice to melt.

Of course, what happened was that some friends organized a spur-of-the-moment trip to Las Vegas and naturally I had to go with them. They were in a big hurry, so instead of waiting for the ice to melt, I put the bowl in the microwave—and guess what happened?

I melted my credit cards.

I swear this is true. I'm laughing as I type this because it's so dumb. I also tried the trick where you leave your credit cards in your car when you go shopping. All this did was make me get all hot and sweaty when I went running back to my car to retrieve them. Cutting up my cards didn't work either. When my cards expired, the card companies sent me new ones. I couldn't help myself—I activated them and went back to charging up a storm.

If this sounds like the behavior of an addict—well, that's what it was. In college, credit cards were like a drug for me. I literally couldn't stop using them.

What changed? One day the bills arrived in the mail and

I was too afraid to open the envelopes. I finally opened them with my eyes closed and my heart racing. When I managed to open my eyes and saw the numbers inside, I almost got sick. How had I done this to myself? This was INSANE.

That was the day I woke up to the truth. The truth was that I was spending money I didn't have to buy things I didn't need. None of the things I was buying were "life necessary." I was rationalizing my overspending. I wanted to be out of debt, and the only way I would ever get there was to STOP SPENDING MONEY.

MY GRANDMA ROSE SET ME STRAIGHT

Around this time, I went to see my grandmother Rose Bach. Grandma Rose had always been one of my money mentors, and I told her all about how stressed I was about my credit card debt. To be honest, I was half hoping she would help me out. Instead of giving me money, however, she gave me advice.

"David," she said, "you want to be rich someday, true?"

"Yes, Grandma," I replied. "I want to be a millionaire by the time I'm 30."

"Well, then," she said, "let me give you some simple advice. You can't out-earn your debt."

I must have looked puzzled, because she smiled and said, "There are rich people every day going broke and there are middle-class people getting rich. Your grandmother is an example of a self-made middle-class woman who became a millionaire because she saved money, she invested—and, above all, she never, ever spent money on anything if she couldn't afford to pay cash for it." She looked at me sternly. "David, you are a smart guy, but you need to grow up. You're about to graduate from college. My advice to you is knock it off. Stop spending money you don't have. Cut up your credit cards for good, pay them off—and never go back. When you get out of college live like you are poor—so in ten years you can actually be rich. Remember: it's not how much you make that will determine whether or not you become wealthy. *It's how much you spend.*"

I LISTENED TO MY GRANDMA— YOU SHOULD, TOO

Grandma Rose always knew how to get through to me. For the rest of my time in college, I stopped using my credit cards. In fact, it took me nearly two full years to pay off all of my credit card debt. And from then on, I used only a debit card and a single charge card (one that did not allow me to carry a balance but rather required me to pay it off in full every month). I'm now in my forties, and this method has worked for me for more than two decades now. I have not had any credit card debt since my early twenties.

Equally if not more important, I have also constantly tried to spend less than I earn. What my grandmother made me realize was that debt reduction equals wealth. I can't tell you I did this all perfectly. I have shared in other books how I also leased a fancy car at a young age and rented an apartment. But over time, Grandma Rose's lecture never left me—and I did become a millionaire by the age of 30.

The basic lesson that my grandmother drilled into my head was, as she said, a simple one—and it's one I want you to think about (and discuss with your spouse or partner if you are married or in a committed relationship where you share finances): The only way out of a debt hole is to stop digging.

Okay—enough sermonizing. Now let's get started on my do-it-yourself system for getting out of debt. As I said earlier, all you need is a pen or pencil, a sheet or two of paper—and the desire to be Debt Free For Life.

> ### DEBT FREE FOR LIFE ACTION STEPS
>
> ❑ Acknowledge that you can't become debt free if you keep piling on debt.
> ❑ Stop spending money you don't have on things you don't need.
> ❑ Try to spend less than you earn.

CHAPTER FIVE

THE DOLP® METHOD:
HOW TO PAY DOWN YOUR DEBT
IN RECORD TIME

So you're ready to get going, aren't you? Good, because now I'm going to share with you a system to pay off your debts that is so simple you can be up and running with it in less than an hour.

Yes, you read that correctly! If you follow the instructions I am about to lay out for you, in less than one hour you will have a foolproof system to pay off everything you owe once and for all.

The system is called DOLP®, short for Done On Last Payment. (In my previous books, I wrote that DOLP stood for "Dead On Last Payment," but readers suggested that "Done" was more motivating than "Dead"—so I have changed it.) The DOLP system is the cornerstone of your Debt Free For Life Plan. I've been talking about DOLP for well over a decade now. I've taught it to millions of people on shows like *Oprah Winfrey* and NBC's *Today,* and through numerous appearances on ABC, CBS, Fox, and other TV networks. I've also described it in a few of my previous books. There's a good reason why I've stuck with the DOLP system all these years: it's simple and *it works.*

Are you ready? Great—let's go.

GET STARTED ORGANIZING YOUR DEBT

The first step in DOLPing your way out of debt is to get organized. It's a lot like getting on a scale before you start a diet.
You have to step right up, open your eyes, look down—and
face the truth.

Debt is something you need to see in black and white. You
can't expect your Debt Free For Life Plan to work—and you
won't be able to measure your progress each month as you pay
down your debt—unless you start off knowing exactly how
much you owe.

Are you excited? You should be. You're about to change
your whole life.

GO GET YOUR CREDIT CARD STATEMENTS

To start the process of getting your debt organized, the first
thing you need to do is go and get all the statements and other
documents from every credit card account you have. Then go
and get some folders. (Ideally, they should be red so they will
stand out in your file drawer.) Now create a file for each different credit card account and label it appropriately (e.g., "Visa
Credit Card"). From now on, you will put all of your statements and payment receipts for this particular account in this
particular folder.

On the front of each folder, I want you to write with a big
black marker the total amount of debt you currently owe on a
card. Make the numbers big and bold so you can instantly see in
black and white how big this particular debt is, and next to this
figure write down today's date. Each time you make a payment
that reduces this credit card debt, you will cross out the old total
and below it write down the new, smaller total you owe.

In this way, you will automatically create a handwritten journal that keeps track of how your debt is shrinking. Just seeing a record—*in your own handwriting*—of the progress you are making each month is going to motivate you as never before.

In a few minutes, you are going to take this information about your credit card debt and start filling out the DOLP Worksheet on page 62. But for now I want you to do the simple arithmetic needed to complete the short credit card worksheet below.

FIGURE OUT HOW MANY CREDIT CARDS YOU HAVE

Number of credit cards I have: _____

Number of credit cards my spouse/partner has: _____

Number of credit cards my kids (or other dependents) have: _____

Total number of credit cards my whole family has: _____

The total amount of debt we carry on these credit cards is $_____

The total monthly minimum payment due is $_____

To figure out the totals, use the worksheet that follows. List each credit card account and its current outstanding balance, starting with the smallest debt and working down to the largest. In this way you will figure out exactly how much you owe and who you owe it to.

DEBT REALITY WORKSHEET				
Name of Creditor	Account Number	Outstanding Balance	Monthly Minimum Payment	Interest Rate
1.				
2.				
3.				
4.				
5.				
6.				
7.				
8.				
9.				
10.				
11.				
12.				
13.				

NOW FIGURE OUT ALL YOUR OTHER DEBTS

Once you've filed all your credit card statements and added up your totals, it's time to add up all the other debt you have—mortgages, car loans, student loans, everything. To begin with, I want you to gather up all the statements for your mortgage and related debts, such as second (or third) mortgages and home-equity loans. As you did before, create a file for each debt, label it (e.g., "Wells Fargo home mortgage"), and on the front of the folder write the total amount you currently owe. Do the same for any car loans or other personal loans you may have. Finally, if you still owe money on any student loans, make a file for each of them and write the total current loan balance on the front of the folders.

Now add up all of this other debt and record it as follows.

> I owe $_____ on my primary mortgage.
> I owe $_____ on second mortgages/home equity loans, etc.
> I owe $_____ on second property/vacation homes or rental properties.
> I owe $_____ on student loans.
> I owe $_____ on car loans/boat loans.
> I owe $_____ on other installment debt.
>
> The total amount of additional debt I carry is $_____.
>
> The Grand Total I owe as of _____ [today's date] is $_____.

ADDING UP ALL OF YOUR DEBT ISN'T FUN— BUT IT IS HELPFUL

I'm not going to pretend that what I have just asked you to do won't hurt. Having coached literally thousands of people on this process, I can't tell you the number of times I have seen someone almost go into shock when they see in black and white how much they really owe and to how many different banks and companies. For many people, completing this exercise is the first time they've ever gotten a good look at how deep in debt they actually are.

I once went through this process with a couple on a television show, and they were stunned to discover that they owed nearly twice what they had "guesstimated." They went on the show thinking they had about $40,000 in debt. In fact, the total turned out to be $72,000. I'll never forget the look on their faces when I showed them the final figure.

It was not a pleasant experience for them. But here's the reality of the situation—**you can't cure what you don't face.** The number-one mistake I see people making with their debt is what I call "debt denial." There's a dangerous attitude many of us have that can be summed up in the phrase: "If I don't see it, it's not real."

This is why so many people who are behind on debt payments don't even bother to open up the envelopes when their statements come in the mail. I'm sure this isn't you—but I am also willing to bet that you don't know exactly how much debt you currently have. Which is why this step, as simple as it is, is so critical.

LET'S ROLL UP OUR SLEEVES
AND BE HONEST WITH OURSELVES

According to the Federal Reserve, the average American family carries credit card balances totaling nearly $17,000. And that's just the average. In my experience as a "money coach" for nearly two decades, I have seen firsthand that when it comes to credit cards many of us operate way, way above average. Both on Oprah's "Debt Diet" series and on the weekly "Money 911" segments I did for the *Today* show, I have met and worked with people who had run up $25,000, $50,000, $75,000—even more than $100,000—in credit card debt.

There's a classic twist on the old song that the Seven Dwarfs sang in Disney's *Snow White*: "I owe, I owe—so it's off to work I go." It's a cute line, but is that really what you want? I don't think so. In fact, I know you don't. If you did, you wouldn't be reading this book. So let's roll up our sleeves, be honest with ourselves, and deal once and for all with how much debt we really have.

Use the Debt Reality Worksheet to total everything up.

DOLPING YOUR WAY OUT OF DEBT

Now that your debt is organized and you have all of your records in front of you, it's time to fill out the DOLP Worksheet. As I told you earlier, the DOLP system is the method I have taught for more than a decade to help people create an action plan that will get them out of debt. The process is simple, straightforward, and can be completed in less than an hour. In fact, if you have already done all the chores I said you needed to do up to this point, then you are pretty much done with the bulk of the work involved in creating a DOLP plan. All you really need to do now to get your "fast-pay plan" on paper is simply plug in your debt numbers.

The entire purpose of the DOLP plan is to build what I call debt-reduction momentum. In particular, it's about getting your credit card accounts paid down and "gone." By gone, I mean you have paid the cards off—and, ideally, have stopped carrying any debt on them. This is what I mean when I say you are going to DOLP your debts away—you are going to make sure your credit card and other loan accounts are Done On Last Payment. (I don't mean you should close the accounts. As you will see in Chapter Eight when I discuss your credit score, you should probably keep them open to keep your credit score up.)

So here's how you do it.

1. Fill out the DOLP Worksheet.

Your DOLP Worksheet will become the "scale" that you will use to track how much total debt all your various loans add up to—and in which order you should pay them off. You'll find both a blank worksheet and a sample worksheet on pages 62–63. In addition, there's an interactive version online at **www. finishrich.com/dolp**. Whichever one you use, filling it out is really easy. In the first column, you simply write in the name of the loan account. In the next column, you put the balance you owe, followed by the minimum payment due. The fourth column is for the payment due date. For the moment, hold off on filling this in. The last two columns are for the loan's DOLP Number and its DOLP Ranking. These two items are the heart of the DOLP system, and figuring them out (which we'll do next) is super easy.

DOLP® WORKSHEET					
Account	Outstanding Balance	Minimum Monthly Payment	Payment Due Date	DOLP Number (Balance/Min Payment)	DOLP Ranking

				SAMPLE DOLP WORKSHEET	
Account	Outstanding Balance	Minimum Monthly Payment	Payment Due Date	DOLP Number (Balance/Min Payment)	DOLP Ranking
Visa	$500	$50	10th of the month	10	1
MasterCard	$775	$65	15th of the month	12	2
Discover Card	$1,150	$35	1st of the month	39	3

2. Calculate the DOLP Number for each account.

To figure out each account's DOLP Number, you simply divide the outstanding balance by the minimum monthly payment. For example, if you owe $500 on Visa and your minimum payment is $50, you would take the $500 and divide it by $50, which would give your Visa account a DOLP Number of 10. The 10 represents how many monthly minimum payments (not counting interest) it would take to pay off your debt. After you've finished calculating a DOLP Number for all of your credit card accounts, do the same for your other debts. Keep in mind that with most closed-end loans, such as home mortgages, student loans, and car loans, you can find the number of payments left listed on your statements. If it's not there, leave the space for the DOLP Number blank. We'll come back to them later.

3. Assign each account a DOLP Ranking.

This is even easier than calculating the DOLP Number. The account with the lowest DOLP Number is ranked #1, the account with the second lowest is ranked #2, and so on. The table on page 63 shows you an example of how this might look.

---

4. Calendar your due dates.

Now I want you to fill in the "payment due date" column in the worksheet for all of your loans, credit card and otherwise. While you are at it, I also want you to add these due dates to whatever calendar system you use—whether it's on your computer (like Microsoft Outlook) or online (like Google Calendar) or on your desk (like an old-fashioned Day-at-a-Glance diary). Regardless of the technology involved, set your calendar to remind you of all your payment due dates at least five days ahead of time. This should prevent you from making any late payments—and thus making your situation even worse by getting hit with costly late fees. You can protect yourself even more by signing up with your credit card companies to receive an email alert when your bill is coming due. Also, once you've got all your due dates written down right in front of you, it's really easy to figure out how you might rearrange them so they all come at the most convenient time for you (whether that's all at once or bunched twice a month). Most credit card companies and many other lenders will work with you to change their due dates for this very reason.

---

5. Fast-pay your debt—the DOLP way.

Now that your DOLP Worksheet is completely filled out, you're ready to start DOLPing your way out of debt. What the DOLP system does is tell you which of your loans you should pay off first in order to become debt free as quickly as possible. Here's what you do. Each month, you make the

minimum payment on every credit card account you have . . .
EXCEPT the one with the lowest DOLP Ranking. For that
card, you make as big a payment as you can manage. Ideally,
this payment should be at least **double** the minimum payment. Using the examples in the sample worksheet on page
63, you would pay $65 to MasterCard, $35 to Discover Card,
and at least $100 to Visa. Once a card has been paid off com-
pletely (you've DOLPed it—it's dead—hooray!), you bury it
(which is to say you put it in a drawer, cut it up, etc.) and start
attacking the account with the next lowest DOLP Ranking—
in the example on page 63, the MasterCard.

THE DOLP SYSTEM:
A PROVEN STRATEGY TO PAY DOWN DEBT

By creating a DOLP list of your debts, you now know which of
your credit cards can and should be paid off fastest! The DOLP
system works because it helps you to quickly identify the card
you can realistically pay off with the fewest payments. And
once that card is paid off, you can put that much more toward
paying off the card with the next-lowest DOLP ranking. As
each card is paid off, you have more money left to pay off your
remaining cards. Seems easy, right? The truth is that the system *is* easy. It's simply a matter of prioritizing your debts and
then fast-paying the right card down.

One question I am often asked is how much more than the
minimum payment you should make to the card with the
lowest DOLP Ranking. As I said above, I recommend you
try to pay at least twice the minimum payment—but more
is always better, because more means you will get the card
paid off faster. And take it from me, if you haven't already

experienced this yourself, there is nothing like the feeling you get when you check off a debt as paid in full. Hopefully, it won't be too long before you've got your #1 DOLP card paid off and you can start making extra payments on your #2 DOLP card. I have coached people who in less than a year were able to pay off more than a half dozen credit card balances. Each time they retired a card, they celebrated (inexpensively).

That said, you shouldn't be under any illusions. DOLPing takes time, effort, and commitment. You've got to be realistic about this. It probably took you years to get into debt, so don't expect that you'll be able to get out of it in a few months. Several years is a more likely time frame. But don't be discouraged. Your progress may be slower than you'd like, but with your new-found knowledge, plan, and willingness to take action, it will be steady.

WHY IT'S SO IMPORTANT TO
REDUCE THE NUMBER OF CARDS YOU HAVE

The point of DOLPing your debt is to *reduce the number of credit card balances you are carrying—fast*. Using this method achieves this goal much faster than, say, focusing on the highest interest rate.

Reducing the number of different credit card debts you have is MISSION NUMBER ONE. Why? Because the more balances you carry, the greater the chance there is that you will be late on a payment or go over a credit limit—and get hit with huge penalty fees. Penalty fees are the bread and butter of the credit card industry. In many cases, credit card companies make more money from penalty and administrative fees than from interest charges. The fact is that a small card with even a small balance can cost you an absolute fortune. If you miss a payment on your "small card" with a $500 balance, the late fee could be as much as $50. If you kept using that card (and, again, you're not going to, right?) and you went over your credit limit, the penalty fee could be $100. Imagine—if you were late and went over the limit, the fee for the month would be $150!

This is why when it comes to getting out of debt fast, there are more important factors than interest rates. And by the way, the credit card companies built their business on this exact premise.

USING DOLP—WITHOUT HAVING TO DO ANY OF THE WORK

Now don't get me wrong. I'm not saying that interest rates don't matter at all. They do—and later on in this book, in Chapter Seven, I will show you how you can get the credit card companies to lower your rates. But first I want to share with you a new online tool that allows you to use the DOLP system without having to do any of the work yourself. It's called Debt Wise, and I created it with Equifax, the world's leading credit reporting company. What Debt Wise does is automatically gather all your debt information and figure out your DOLP Rankings in minutes.

DEBT FREE FOR LIFE ACTION STEPS

❏ Create a file system for all your credit card accounts.
❏ Use the Debt Reality Worksheet to figure out how much debt you have and whom you owe it to.
❏ Fill out the DOLP Worksheet and use the information in it to prioritize your debts by DOLP Number, or use the free online DOLP Worksheet at **www.finishrich.com/dolp**.
❏ Start fast-paying your debts the DOLP way.

CHAPTER SIX

GET OUT OF DEBT AUTOMATICALLY WITH DEBT WISE

You've just learned how to use my DOLP system to get out of debt. Again, I have taught this approach to millions of people. It's proven to be simple and effective. The only catch is that you have to do the work. You have to input your debt and constantly update your progress.

Maybe you would rather not do all this work yourself. If so, you're in luck! There is now a revolutionary web-based product that will do all this for you. It's called Debt Wise, and it is the first tool of its kind that lets you manage your debt from the comfort of your home by accessing your credit file through your home computer. In a nutshell, Debt Wise does exactly what I teach with DOLP—only it does it automatically, including updating your progress! What's more, it is safe and secure, and it will take you about or as little as ten minutes to get started using it.

Equifax, the company that built Debt Wise, says the average person who uses it can expect to save more than $30,000 in interest charges on their credit cards, other loans, and mortgages, and get out of debt 15 years quicker. In fact, this is a conservative estimate. The truth is that for many of you, the savings could be much, much higher. But I am getting ahead of myself. Let's start by going through exactly what Debt Wise will do for you and why I got involved with this totally revolutionary tool to get you out of debt.

WHY I LOVE DEBTWISE.COM—
AND WHY YOU WILL, TOO

Equifax is a leading U.S. credit bureau, a publicly traded company (stock symbol: EFX) that has been in business for more than 100 years. It launched Debt Wise back in 2009, and as soon as I saw this new debt-reduction tool, I just about flipped out with excitement.

I was at my computer in my office and had clicked on what must have been one of the first banner ads they had put up online for the product. "Wow!" I exclaimed. I called over my team. "Guys," I said. "You will not believe this! Someone has just launched a new product to get America out of debt that does exactly what I have been teaching for over a decade— only it's even better because it's totally AUTOMATIC!"

My team gathered around my monitor. "Seriously, look at this!" I continued. "Someone has taken my DOLP system and put it online. Only it's better than that because it does all the work for you! This tool allows you to import all of your debt information from your credit file—it pulls in every loan balance you have, whether it's from a credit card, mortgage, car loan, student loan, or whatever, and then it automatically helps you prioritize the order in which you should pay them down!"

My team had two reactions to this: "Wow, that's amazing!" and "Why didn't we think of this?"

"Yes, it is amazing," I said, "and that's a good question."

Once we had figured out that Equifax was behind Debt Wise, we understood why we couldn't have done it ourselves. Of course, we couldn't do what Equifax had done. There's no way we could develop a tool that accesses people's credit records automatically. Only one of the big three credit bureaus would have this data.

THE BEST TOOL EVER TO GET OUT OF DEBT— AUTOMATICALLY!

I just couldn't believe it! I immediately launched the Debt Wise tutorial in order to try it myself. (You can do this yourself at **www.DebtWise.com**.) This may sound strange, but being that personal finance is what I do, I literally felt like a kid in a candy store. "This is it!" I said to my team. "It's the 'Holy Grail' of how to get out of debt."

For years I had been showing Americans how to pay themselves first—AUTOMATICALLY. I had written a #1 *New York Times* bestseller called *The Automatic Millionaire* that taught millions of people how to build wealth automatically, without a budget or relying on self-discipline. But automatic debt reduction was always a problem. There was no way I knew of to make "paying it off" truly automatic. Until now. Now Debt Wise had provided the tool.

After two hours of playing with Debt Wise, I knew two things. One, I had to get involved with this product; and two, if I did, together we could change how Americans pay down their debt. We could finally make paying down your debt truly automatic.

To make a long story short, Equifax and I decided to partner together a year later. Working together, we made Debt Wise even better and easier to use, integrating me as your personal coach on the website. Tens of thousands of people have already used the product with great success, and I am beyond excited to share it with you now.

> ### DEBT FREE FOR LIFE SUCCESS STORY
>
> Debt Wise gave me a way of presenting my debt on a dashboard, and I was quickly able to get a handle on what the facts were. I have been able to stay on plan and ahead of some of my financial goals. It is really working, and it reduces the stress knowing that I feel empowered with Debt Wise.
>
> **Alison A.**
> **Seabrook, NH**

DEBT WISE: YOUR ULTIMATE DO-IT-YOURSELF TOOL FOR GETTING OUT OF DEBT!

Here's exactly what Debt Wise will help you do.

- You will be able to calculate your personal **"Debt Freedom Day"** and know exactly *when* you can be out of debt.

- You will learn how to pay down your debt more effectively, by prioritizing which debt to pay down first.

- You will learn how to pay down your debt faster—using the "Fast Pay Plan."

- You will learn how much money this new "Fast Pay Plan" can save you.

- You will be able to monitor your progress safely and securely from the convenience of your home, office, or virtually anywhere you have access to the Internet.

- You will be able to get started doing all this in as little as ten minutes.

- **And you can try it out for FREE!**

Sound exciting? It really is. So now let me explain exactly how Debt Wise works.

SEVEN TOOLS THAT CAN CHANGE YOUR LIFE IN MINUTES!

Debt Wise is the first-ever online product that is powered by YOUR credit report. Because Equifax already has your credit file, it can automatically upload your debt information and create a debt payment plan personalized for you. This book contains a FREE COUPON that allows you to try the program for 30 days at no cost. (Details on how to get it are at the back of the book.)

My suggestion is that you turn to page 81, use the coupon code, and sign up for the free trial—you have nothing to lose.

The Debt Wise website will show you how much the program will cost you after the trial period is up. As of this writing, the cost is 50 cents a day (much, much less than a cup of coffee at your favorite coffee shop).

When you log in to Debt Wise (at **www.debtwise.com**), you will find the following tools:

1. **PLAN SUMMARY—DEBT FREEDOM DAY CALCULA-TOR.** This feature is where it all starts. In one glance, you will know how much debt you have, the amount you are paying, what your debt is costing you, and when you will be debt free (your Debt Freedom Day). The calculator will also show how much money you can save by using the FAST PAY PLAN.

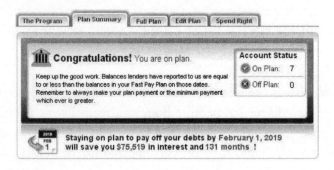

2. **FAST PAY PLAN WIZARD.** This tool makes setting up your plan simple, straightforward, and flexible. It automatically imports your debt data from your Equifax Credit Report and enables you to add debts to the payment plan that Equifax may not have in its records (say, a personal loan from a friend or relative).

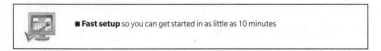

3. **AUTOMATIC MONITORING AND ALERTS.** With this feature, you will know if you are on plan or off plan and when an account is paid off—all automatically! Plus, if anything changes on your Equifax credit file, you will be notified within 24 hours.

■ **Monitoring and Alerts** help you know if you are *on or off plan*, when you've paid off an account, or if there are key changes to your Equifax credit file

4. **EQUIFAX CREDIT SCORES.** This tool allows you to check your Equifax Credit Score and watch it throughout the year to see how paying down your debt impacts your score over time.

■ **Four Equifax Credit Scores** every 12 months - so you can check your credit score as it may change over time

5. **COMMITMENT CALCULATOR.** With this tool, you can look at how making additional payments will speed up your debt reduction and help you get to your Debt Freedom Day faster.

■ **Commitment Calculator** tool to see how paying additional amounts towards your debts could allow you to accelerate your debt freedom date

6. **SPEND RIGHT TOOLS.** Here you will find videos and great articles on ways to save money and spend smarter. I've added my Latte Factor Calculator to this section so you can see how little expenses add up and how you can save a fortune on just a few dollars a day. Millions have used this tool—I think you will love it.

 ■ **Spend Right** tools and tips to help you stay on track

DEBT FREE FOR LIFE SUCCESS STORY

When I started using Debt Wise, I had acquired several credit cards. I tried to pay them down but the balances just never seemed to change. Then I found out about Debt Wise. At first, I was a little skeptical, but now I've paid off quite a few of my credit cards and I'm on track to pay them all off. I couldn't have done it without the help of Debt Wise. Thank you!

Melissa W.
Galloway, New Jersey

THE DEBT-STACKING TOOL
THAT MAKES DOLP AUTOMATIC!

The thing I love most about Debt Wise is the tool that shows what they call "Debt Stacking." Debt Stacking is really another way of saying DOLPing. Debt Wise's tool creates your DOLP Plan—the order in which you pay down your various debts—automatically. It not only assembles all the information for you, but it also does all of the math. It helps you see in black and white which debt should be paid off the fastest so you know which debt to apply extra payments to. Here is a graphic that shows you what this tool looks like.

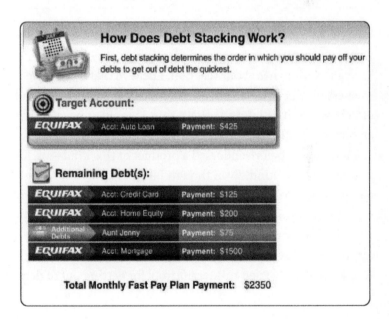

YOUR DO-IT-YOURSELF
DEBT-REDUCTION DASHBOARD

When you log in to Debt Wise, you will see a screen, called the dashboard, that contains everything you need to know about your debt, including your Debt Freedom Day. Among other things, it displays your credit score, you can review your credit score (you get four scores a year with your membership), and you can see how it is doing. Pretty cool, right?

TAKE THE FREE TEST DRIVE
AND FIND OUT FOR YOURSELF

Don't take my word for any of this. Try it out yourself and see what you think.

I can't wait to hear your reaction. I believe that Debt Wise is the best product available anywhere today to help you get out of debt yourself. If I didn't believe this, I wouldn't have associated myself with it!

I have never before endorsed a product of this kind—or, for that matter, any kind. Even though I have had many strategic partnerships over the years, this is the first time I have put my name, face, brand, and reputation behind a particular product. That's how much I believe in Debt Wise. So please take a test drive and see what you think. Join the tens of thousands who have already tried this terrific tool for getting out of debt.

DEBT FREE FOR LIFE SUCCESS STORY

Debt Wise has keep me focused on paying down my bills faster and it flagged me when I was about to go off track. I am so thankful that I have this tool to help myself with my debt.

Charlene D.
Atlanta, GA

HOW SAFE IS DEBT WISE?

The biggest question you may have—and it's one I certainly had—is how safe and secure is Debt Wise?

The answer is that it's safer than anything out there today when it comes to tracking your debt online. All of the current web-based programs that track your expenses and/or your debt require you to input your information and provide them with the passwords to your various accounts so they can access your data. Candidly, many of the free programs out there worry me. What if their tools are not secure?

With Debt Wise, you're not requesting any data from other sources. For instance, you're not giving permission to share your credit card information with anyone. Because Equifax is one of the big three credit bureaus, the issuing bank for Visa already tells them what is going on with your credit card. Every time you borrow money or make a loan payment, the credit card companies and the banks report it to Equifax automatically.

So Equifax already has all of your information locked safely in its databases. Through Debt Wise, it simply shows you the same data that's in your credit report and reflected in your credit score—only you're seeing it in an easy-to-understand format designed to help you create and track a super-effective debt-reduction plan.

REAL PEOPLE WHO'VE ALREADY HAD REAL SUCCESS

You've already seen a few testimonials about how well this program works—and you can read more of them at DebtWise. com. But don't take anyone's word for it—even mine. Take advantage of the one-month free trial that comes with this book (you can find details at **www.finishrich.com/debtwise** and on the next page). Then let us know how you do.

Now that you've been equipped with the tools you need to start paying off your debts, we are going to look at the big game the credit card companies don't want you to focus on— the outrageous interest rates they are charging you. Once you understand exactly what they are charging, you'll be better prepared to negotiate the interest rates down and find a better deal on your debt.

FREE TRIAL OF DEBT WISE

Debt Free For Life comes with a free one-month trial of **debtwise.com**.

You can go right now to **www.debtwise.com/debtfreeforlife** and then enter the coupon code: **bach30**. The value of this one month trial is $14.95—but your first month trial is FREE. There is a membership fee after the first month trial. All details are found on the website. There are also more details on the program in the back of the book. **This free offer expires 1/1/2012.** Enjoy!

DEBT FREE FOR LIFE ACTION STEPS

❏ Go to **www.DebtWise.com** and try the Debt Wise tutorial.

❏ Go to **www.debtwise.com/debtfreeforlife** and then enter the FREE trial coupon code: **bach30**. There you can sign up for the free trial of Debt Wise for 30 days.

❏ Take the free "test drive" and decide for yourself whether Debt Wise is a great tool for helping you get out of debt.

CHAPTER SEVEN

NEGOTIATE YOUR DEBT DOWN: HOW TO LOWER THE INTEREST RATES ON YOUR CREDIT CARDS

I want you to stop now and take a moment to recognize how far you have come in your Debt Free For Life Plan. You've faced up to your debt, organized it, prioritized it, and learned the math that the credit card companies don't want you to understand. In a short period of time, you've truly come a long way in dealing with your debt.

It's really important that you give yourself credit for the work you have done. Remember, *you* bought this book—*you* opened it, *you* have been reading it. You are doing the work and soul-searching it takes to make better decisions about your future and your money. YOU ARE DEALING with your debt.

I'm not trying to make a "rah-rah" speech here. I'm reminding you of this because dealing with your debt is a lot like exercise. You don't get in shape overnight. It's easy to start anything, but the secret to success is not just starting—it's staying with it.

In this chapter, I am going to share with you a five-step plan to lower the interest rates on your credit cards. While the steps themselves are incredibly simple, I want you to know up front that none of this is a "slam dunk." It used to be much easier to get your credit card rates lowered than it is today. Once upon a time, just threatening to close your account would get a credit card company to give you a better rate. (I actually talked about this in my previous books.) But today, as a result of the recession, the debt meltdown, and the credit crunch, we are living in a different world. It used to be that higher rates were the penalty you paid for being a late payer or having a bad credit card score. But now, for no reason at all, credit card companies are hiking the interest rates they charge even long-time customers. They are also cutting credit limits and closing the accounts of cardholders who don't use them often enough.

Still, I don't want you to be discouraged. Even though the companies are fighting hard to keep interest rates high, people I coach do manage to get their rates lowered every day, and you can too. It will take work, but trust me—it will be worth it.

THE MATH BEHIND HIGH INTEREST RATES— HOW THE CREDIT CARD COMPANIES GET YOU

The basic math of credit card interest rates is staggering. Consider what happened recently to a good friend of mine. Alice and I literally grew up together, and she has been reading my books for years. (It helps that I always give her a free copy.) Not long ago, when I gave her a copy of my last book, she had a story for *me*. "David," she said, "you won't believe what just happened to me with my Citibank AAdvantage Visa card."

The truth is nothing surprises me anymore when it comes to how low the credit card companies will stoop, but Alice's story actually did shock me. (To be honest, I was a little skeptical of her story until I checked it out myself.)

Here's what happened. Alice had been a loyal and responsible user of her Citibank AAdvantage Visa card since 1998. She loved the card because it enabled her to earn so many frequent-flyer points, and she always made her payments on time. While she normally paid off her monthly bill in full, she had recently lost her job and as a result she was currently carrying a balance of about $10,000. Her interest rate had always been rather low—about 9%—but following the advice I gave in my last book, *Start Over, Finish Rich,* she made a point of checking her statement to see what her current rate was. To her shock, she discovered that Citibank was charging her 29%!

"Twenty-nine percent!" she thought. "That can't be. I've never once missed a payment. It must be a mistake."

So she called the phone number on her credit card and asked if the figure she had seen on her statement was in fact correct. Was her rate really 29% or had she misread it?

The customer-service representative who took her call explained that, no, she hadn't misread it. Her rate *was* 29%.

Alice asked how that could be, and the nice customer-service lady explained that Citibank Visa had raised *everyone's* rates to 29%, regardless of their payment record or credit history.

When she got off the phone, Alice did the math. Here's what it looked like.

Alice's Citibank Visa card

$10,000 (interest rate 9%)
Total cost to pay off with 2.5% minimum payment: $14,192

$10,000 (interest rate 29%)
Total cost to pay off with 2.5% minimum payment: $85,547

AT 29% INTEREST, THERE IS A $71,355 DIFFERENCE!

Outrageous, right? Not surprisingly, Alice was mad, really mad. "How can they do that?" she asked me. "And what can I do?"

While not everyone's situation is as difficult as Alice's, what she went through is similar to what millions of people are going through right now. Maybe you are one of them.

I told Alice to bring me her statement and we would call the credit card company together to see what could be done to negotiate her rate down.

Over the next several pages, I am going to share with you what Alice and I did, so you can do exactly the same thing for yourself. Keep in mind that Alice did not achieve instant success in getting her rates lowered. However, she did ultimately make progress, and so can you.

GET YOUR CREDIT CARD COMPANY
TO GIVE YOU A BETTER RATE

The process of getting your interest rates lowered begins with your filling out the Debt Free For Life Negotiator Worksheet on page 87. You will use this worksheet to track the calls—and the progress—you make in negotiating your interest rate down. But before you do anything, I want you to read this section first in its entirety. Then fill out the worksheet and start making calls.

> **1. Find out how much interest you are paying.**

The first thing Alice did was to note the interest rate she was being charged on her credit card debts. If you filled out the DOLP Worksheet on page 62 or used the DebtWise.com online tool, you already have this information. If not, go get your latest credit card statements. Your APR, or Annualized Percentage Rate, should be listed at the very top or the very bottom of the statement. If you can't find it or, like Alice, you

THE DEBT FREE FOR LIFE NEGOTIATOR WORKSHEET
My Current Credit Card Companies

Company	Balance	Current rate	Spoke to:	Offer	Staying/ Going?

New Companies I've Called

Company	What they offered	Accepting/Declining?

My Credit Cards and Rates Going Forward

Credit card #1

Old company _____   New company _____

Old rate _____%   New rate _____%

Credit card #2

Old company _____   New company _____

Old rate _____%   New rate _____%

Credit card #3

Old company _____   New company _____

Old rate _____%   New rate _____%

Credit card #4

Old company _____   New company _____

Old rate _____%   New rate _____%

aren't sure you're reading it right, then call your credit card company and ask them what your APR is. (By the way, if you signed up for a card that offered you a rate "only 10 points above prime," don't think that means your rate is 10%. Your rate is whatever the prime rate happens to be—PLUS another 10%. So if the prime rate is 3.25%, which is where it is as I write this—and has been since December 2008—then your real rate is actually 13.25%. The "only 10 points above prime" phrasing is a trick they use to make you think your rate is lower than it really is—just one more scam the credit card companies have used for years to fool us.)

2. Shop for a lower rate.

The second thing I did with Alice was to have her "Google" all her credit cards (using each card's exact name) and compare the interest rate she was currently paying to the rate each of her card companies was offering to new customers. You should do the same thing now with all of your cards. In Alice's case, we were able to find out in less than five seconds that Citibank Visa was offering new customers who qualified an APR of just 13%, *plus* 30,000 frequent-flyer miles once you charged $750. This is what you call adding insult to injury. Alice had been a Citibank AAdvantage Visa customer for more than a decade, she had never been late making a payment, and she had a good credit score. Yet Citibank had stuck her with an interest rate more than twice as high as what they were offering new customers. This is the type of information you want to know before you get on the phone to ask your credit card company for a lower rate.

3. Compare your rate to national averages.

The beauty of the Internet is how easy it is to shop for interest rates—and to find out if you are being treated fairly. Yet very few people take advantage of this fact. You can get the latest credit card rates, along with national averages, at websites like **www.bankrate.com, www.creditcard.com, www.cardweb. com, www.credit.com,** and **www.lowcards.com.** The credit card companies currently offer five basic kinds of rates, depending on what type of borrower you are: super prime for the most creditworthy; prime for average borrowers; subprime for below-average borrowers; punitive rates for borrowers who have missed payments, are behind on payments, have exceeded their credit limits, or have poor credit scores; and promotional rates for new customers. The following chart from **www.cardtrak.com** shows the different rates for each type of borrower.

FIVE KINDS OF CREDIT CARD RATES

	Jan 2010	Jul 2009	Jan 2009
Super-Prime:	10.59%	9.69%	8.99%
Prime:	15.44%	14.99%	13.77%
Sub-Prime:	26.01%	22.99%	21.67%
Punitive:	29.99%	29.12%	29.99%
Promotional:	5.77%	3.33%	2.66%

Note: Average Rates based on FICO Credit Scores.
Super-Prime = 760–850; Prime = 660–759; Sub-Prime = 500–659.
Source: CardTrak.com

4. Compare your rate to your credit score.

Before you start calling your credit card companies, take a good look at the table on page 89 and determine what category your credit score should qualify you for. If you don't already know your credit score, go to **www.finishrich.com/debtwise** and get your Equifax Credit Score, which is included in your free trial of DebtWise.com. While you can get your credit report for free once a year from each of the major credit bureaus, normally getting your credit *score* on your own, as I discuss in Chapter Eight, would cost you $15.95. If you already registered at DebtWise.com, log in to your account and click on "credit score." (You'll find it right in the middle of your Debt Wise home page.)

We'll cover everything you need to know about credit scores in the next chapter, but obviously if you have a "super prime" borrower's credit score, then your credit card company shouldn't be charging you the regular "prime" rate. If they are, ask them why when you call them. Remember—unless you make the effort to get your interest rates down by asking for a fair deal or a better deal, your rates are going to stay high, and it's going to be harder for you to get out of debt.

OK—are you ready? Great. Let's pick up the phone and start what I call the "Credit Card Rate Negotiation Game."

THE CREDIT CARD RATE NEGOTIATION GAME

You are now ready to negotiate. On the next page, you'll find the Debt Free For Life Rate Negotiator Worksheet. Use it to track your efforts—and your progress.

Negotiating your credit card interest rate can be as easy as simply calling your credit card company and asking, "What's my interest rate on this card—and can I get a better one?" Although this is not always the case, it often is just that simple. A reader of mine named Charlotte recently wrote to me and shared the following story.

David, I can't believe that lowering my rate on my credit cards was as easy as "just asking." I saw you on Oprah discussing this and I did exactly as you said. I carry balances on five credit cards that charge me an average rate of over 20%. Well, I called all five companies, and three of them immediately cut my rate in half! One card offered me zero percent interest for six months if I transferred some new money to them from another card (which I did), and one card refused. Four out of five isn't bad!

The *Wall Street Journal* reported a few years ago that despite all the attention that had been focused on the importance of getting your credit card interest rates reduced, more than 75% of all cardholders hadn't even tried. On the other hand, most of the 25% who did were successful on the first call. Of course, as I said earlier, credit is much tighter today than it used to be, and many credit card companies simply will not give you a lower rate. Even worse, instead of lowering your rates when you ask, some companies will respond by raising them. I share this not to scare you out of trying but to make sure you have all the facts.

As a practical matter, credit card interest rates rarely go beyond 29.99%. So if you're currently paying 25% or more, you really have nothing to lose by asking for a lower rate.

DEBT FREE FOR LIFE SUCCESS STORY

This past weekend my husband and I read *Start Late, Finish Rich.* We are in our fifties so we definitely feel like we are starting late. We had heard about calling to lower our interest rates on our credit cards—but like everyone else, we asked "really?" Well, yesterday, I used your plan and your scripts— and guess what?! It worked! I called my credit card company and asked them about lowering my rate. We'd been paying an outrageous 24.98% forever. The first person I spoke with said she could lower it to 13.9%. I thought to myself, wow— on the first try. Then I thought, why not be courageous and ask for a rate lower than 10%? I asked to be transferred to a supervisor and the next guy asked me some additional ques- tions—and then he said we can lower your rate to 8.96%, starting next month. Amazing—in just five minutes with one call, the rate went down 16%! I was also able to take another card that was charging me a $120 annual fee and 19.5% interest—and with one call switch that to a new card with a $29 annual fee and only 11.5% interest. I am so excited to Finish Rich—even if we are starting late. Thank you!

Bev J.
New York, NY

WHAT IF I ASK FOR A LOWER RATE
AND THEY SAY NO?

When you call the credit card company, your job is to USE YOUR KNOWLEDGE. Remember, you have become smarter about your debt and you now know what kind of rates are being offered, so there's no reason for you to be afraid to ask for a better deal.

When you call a credit card company, you should assume that the first person you speak to is going to say, "Sorry, I can't help you."

This is what the first tier of customer-service reps who take calls are generally trained to say.

If this happens, simply respond by saying, "Well, then let me speak to someone who *can* help me. If you can't work with me on getting a better rate, then please connect me with your supervisor."

When you make this request, the customer-service rep may say, "I'm sorry—no one is available right now." Don't accept this. Again, it's what they are trained to say. Instead, tell them you want their name and ID number, so you have a record of whom you spoke with. Then insist they put a supervisor on the line *immediately*.

Since I first began taking this approach, I have *never* been unable to get a supervisor on the phone. Once you've got him or her on the line, your job is to explain your situation. Start by going over your rate, tell them your credit score, and ask why your rate is higher than it should be. Compare your rate to what competitors are offering and ask if they would be willing to work with you to give you a better deal.

HERE'S WHAT HAPPENED
WITH MY FRIEND ALICE

After researching her card and her credit score, we knew exactly where she stood. Her FICO score was a healthy 740, so based on the chart on page 89, we knew she deserved a "Prime" rate—which at the time was averaging around 15%.

So we called her credit card company. Sure enough, the first person we spoke to said, "Sorry, but there is nothing we can do. We have raised rates across the board. The rate for all our customers with old cards is now 29%."

At that point, we asked to speak with a supervisor. We were immediately transferred to a new representative, a supervisor named Michael. He looked up Alice's payment record and credit history—and immediately offered to lower her 29% rate to 25%. Now, in my opinion, a 4% rate reduction isn't much, especially when the same credit card is being offered to new customers at a fraction of that rate. Looking at this as a challenge, we politely went over the facts again with Michael. He was very friendly and explained that his hands were tied. "Twenty-five percent is truly the best rate we can give you now," he said. Eventually, Alice accepted the 4% reduction and went back to searching for a new card at a lower rate.

Ultimately, Alice wound up taking advantage of an offer she got in the mail—for a card that was offering new customers zero percent interest for six months! She applied and transferred her Citibank Visa balance to it. True, she had to pay a transfer fee of $300, but for six months there wouldn't be any additional charges on her debt. Because she read the fine print on her transfer agreement (something you should always do), she knew that if she were just one day late on even one payment, the rate on her new card would be increased retroactively to 25%. So she made a point not to be late—ever!

SOMETIMES IT'S EASIER
TO LOWER YOUR RATE

In Alice's case, before we gave up on Citibank, we asked Michael if we could speak with *his* supervisor, and he transferred us to the floor manager. He too said he was unable to do anything for Alice. But this isn't always the case. Sometimes, the second or third supervisor has more authority and can lower the rate even when his subordinates say it's impossible. I know this sounds ridiculous, but it is truly a game!

The reality is that there is almost always something they can do. What you need to know is that the credit card companies lower rates all of the time, every day of the year, every hour of the day! On the *Oprah* "Debt Diet" show, I worked with one couple that had 12 credit cards, and we were able to ultimately get all but one of them to lower their rates to below 5%. In some cases it took multiple calls, but the effort paid off in the end.

DEBT FREE FOR LIFE SUCCESS STORY

David, I saw you on television talking about how you can pay down your debts faster when you negotiate with the credit card companies and get your rate lowered. Truthfully, I doubted it would work—but I also figured, what do I have to lose? I had seven credit cards—and I followed your advice exactly as you shared it. Four of the seven credit card companies lowered my interest rate on the first call! One credit card company lowered my rate from 24% to 14%! Another credit card was at 14% and it was lowered to below 10%. Three credit card companies refused, and one even raised my rate. So I took your advice and shopped for a new credit card. In the end, I moved my balances to a card that was offering new customers zero percent interest for six months. I figured out that these calls will save me over $1,000 in interest payments in just the first year! Who knew that a few phone calls could put back so much money in my pocket? Thank you so much for your invaluable advice and for your motivation! And I'm

not giving up on the two card companies that said "no"—I
plan to call them back in 90 days, as you suggested.

Veronica M.
New York, NY

ASK THE CREDIT CARD COMPANIES ABOUT THEIR FORBEARANCE OR DEBT MANAGEMENT PLANS

When all else fails, there is one last resort that can ultimately
get your rates lowered. It's a service that the credit card companies don't actively promote aimed at what they categorize
as "hardship" cases.

The credit card companies know that millions of their customers are in financial distress. It may be because you lost a
job, had an illness in your family, or are simply earning less
than you used to earn (what they call being "underemployed").
What the credit card companies will often do in such cases
is review your situation, and based on what they find, they
may decide to work with you to restructure your debt. This
restructuring can include lowering your interest rates to zero
for a period of time (usually six months to a year), lowering
your minimum payments, suspending over-the-limit penalties or annual fees—or all of the above.

There are two basic types of hardship plans for people
with credit card problems, what are known as "Forbearance
Plans" and what are called "Debt Management Plans (or DMP
Plans)." I have coached people who had credit cards with interest rates as high as 29% who were able to get their rates cut
to zero as a result of signing up for one of these plans. As I

write this in the summer of 2010, the average rates for these plans range from 0% to 9%.

HOW FORBEARANCE PROGRAMS WORK

Millions of credit card customers have taken advantage of these plans. As of the beginning of 2010, Citibank alone had 1.6 million customers enrolled in its forbearance programs. So trust me on this—if you apply and are accepted, you will not be alone.*

In most cases, the first thing you will have to do is explain your "hardship" so the bank can decide whether or not you qualify for the program. If you qualify, they will work out a new payment plan for you. You will then be asked to sign an agreement that commits you to the plan. Read the paperwork closely! The minimum monthly payment will be debited from your checking account, and your credit account will be frozen. This means you can't use it anymore—which is probably a good thing if you are in debt to the point you need one of these plans.

One downside of enrolling in a forbearance program is that your credit card company may report this fact to the credit bureaus—and if they do, your credit score could go down. But not all the card companies report borrowers who enroll in forbearance programs. To find out whether yours does or not, make sure you read the fine print before you sign the contract.

The truth is that even if enrolling in a forbearance program affects your credit score in the short term, it's better than falling behind on your payments or not being able to reduce your

---

*www.citibank.com/citi/press2010/100315a_en.pdf

debt because you're paying so much in interest. And if you can't afford to pay off your cards, you will be hurting your credit score anyway.

HOW DEBT MANAGEMENT PLANS WORK

In addition to forbearance plans, credit card companies offer what are known as Debt Management Plans, or DMPs. We'll cover these more fully in Chapter Twelve, but for now what you need to know is that the primary difference between a forbearance plan and a DMP is the amount of time you have to be in the plan, how much time you have to pay down your debt, and whether the plan will be set up directly with the credit card company or run through a non-profit credit-counseling agency. As a rule, the credit card company will discuss your situation with you and then decide if they feel you are a good candidate for a DMP. If you are judged suitable, they will likely lower your interest rates and waive fees as long as you make the payments required by the plan. In many cases, credit card companies may recommend a DMP—but suggest you work with a non-profit credit counselor in order to qualify. I will explain in detail how to work with a non-profit credit-counseling organization in Chapter Twelve.

DON'T BE DISCOURAGED
IF YOU CAN'T DO IT YOURSELF

If you've managed to get control of your credit card debt by following the steps in this chapter, congratulations! You've come a long way.

But if you haven't managed to do it yourself, don't be discouraged. Not everyone is successful at doing this himself or herself. Lots of people want a professional to help them through this process. Later on, in Chapters Twelve and Thirteen, we'll explore the world of professional credit counselors, how they work, and how you can find one you can trust. Right now, however, let's focus on one of the most important aspects of your financial life—your all-important credit score and the credit reports it is based on.

DEBT FREE FOR LIFE ACTION STEPS

❑ Give yourself credit for how far you have come in your Debt Free For Life Plan.
❑ Fill out the Debt Free For Life Negotiator Worksheet on page 87.
❑ Find out how much interest you're paying on your credit cards and shop around for a better rate.
❑ If necessary, play the Credit Card Rate Negotiation Game.
❑ If you're really in distress, find out about Forbearance and Debt Management Plans.

CHAPTER EIGHT

YOUR CREDIT REPORT AND SCORE: WHAT IT IS AND HOW TO FIX IT FAST

Today, I want you to check your credit report and your credit score. After you finish reading this chapter, I want you to put this book down and go online and pull your credit reports from all three credit bureaus. Then I want you to pull your credit score.

By law, you are entitled to a free copy of your credit reports (I will show you how to get them), and this book comes with a coupon for a free credit score from Equifax as a gift to you. So no excuses. Today is the day you find out exactly what your credit reports say and what your credit score number is. The median credit score in America today is around 720. Yours may be lower or higher. Whichever it is, today is the day I want you to face up to it—and begin to work on improving it (regardless of where it is) and protecting it! This chapter will be your guide to getting all of this done.

WHY YOUR CREDIT REPORTS ARE SO IMPORTANT

People talk about your "credit score" all the time. What they often forget is that what makes up your credit score is based on data from your credit report. As the old programmer's saying goes, garbage in, garbage out. If the information in your report is inaccurate, your score will be, too. And studies have shown that more than 79% of people's credit reports contain errors. Indeed, according to a survey by the National Association of State Public Interest Research Groups, one in four credit reports contain a mistake serious enough to keep you from getting a loan, credit card, or in some cases a job.

So it's vitally important that you check out your credit reports and get any errors corrected as quickly as possible. Fortunately, it's fairly easy to get a free copy of your report and fairly easy to correct any errors you may find in it. Each bureau now has tools on their websites (which you'll find below) to get mistakes corrected online.

HOW TO PULL YOUR CREDIT REPORT—FOR FREE

Under the Fair Credit Reporting Act, the three big credit bureaus (Equifax, Experian, and TransUnion) are required to provide every consumer who asks with a free copy of their credit report once a year. You can get yours by going online to a website the three companies jointly sponsor at **www.annualcreditreport.com**. You can also mail in a request to Annual Credit Report Request Service at P.O. Box 105281, Atlanta, GA 30348-5281 or call them toll-free at (877) 322-8228. (For details about your rights under the FCRA, the Federal Trade Commission has a brochure entitled "Your Access to Free Credit Reports" at **www.ftc.gov/bcp/menus/consumer/credit/rights.shtm**.)

Each of the three credit bureaus has its own database with its own file of information about you, So you need to look at the reports from all three to make sure that the information each has about you is correct and at least comes close to matching what the other bureaus have.

HOW TO GET THOSE ERRORS CORRECTED

Among other things, the Fair Credit Reporting Act requires both the credit-reporting agencies and the banks and merchants that provide them with data to correct inaccurate or incomplete information in your report when it's pointed out to them and can be proven. By law, once you request a correction from a credit bureau, it must respond within 30 days. Normally, the credit bureau will take your correction or complaint to the company that you believe has made an error and ask them for additional information. If you have proof that an error was made, you can expedite things by providing it to both the bureau and the company you are complaining about.

It is critical you do this work with all three bureaus when you find an error. Fixing an error at Equifax won't correct it at Experian or TransUnion. They are all separate companies that compete with each other, and they do not share information.

All three credit bureaus recommend you use the correction forms on their websites, rather than sending in your complaint via regular mail. But if you feel more comfortable sending them a registered letter than relying on an online form, here is a sample letter you can use as a model. (The mailing address of each bureau is listed afterward.)

[Insert Date]
[Insert Name of Credit Agency]

[Insert Address]

RE: Request to correct errors in credit report #[insert your credit report's file number.]

Dear [insert agency's name]:

In reviewing the credit report you sent me on [insert date], I have noticed the following errors:

1. [Describe the first error—e.g., "You list my date of birth as Jan. 1, 1900."]

This is incorrect. The correct information is: [be very specific here and accompany it with proof if you have it—e.g., "As the enclosed copy of my birth certificate shows, my date of birth is July 25, 1963."].

2. [Describe the second error—e.g., "You list me as having an active charge account with Sears."]

This is incorrect. The correct information is: [be very specific here and accompany it with proof if you have it—e.g., "I closed this account on March 15, 2001. Please note the enclosed copy of the letter I sent Sears instructing them to close the account."].

3. [Describe the third error—e.g., "You list me as having made two late payments on my Bank of America home mortgage."]

This is incorrect. The correct information is: [be very specific here and accompany it with proof if you have it—e.g., "I have made all my mortgage payments on time. Please note the enclosed copy of my latest mortgage statement as well as a letter from Bank of America confirming this fact."].

According to the Fair Credit Reporting Act, you are required to respond to my request within 30 days. My contact information is: [insert your mailing address and phone number].

Sincerely yours,

[Insert your name]

The contact information for the big-three credit-reporting agencies is as follows.

Equifax Information Services, LLC
P.O. Box 740241
Atlanta, GA 30374
(800) 685-1111
www.equifax.com
You can file a dispute online at **www.ai.equifax.com/Credit-Investigation/jsp/ECC_Dispute_Login.jsp.**

Experian
888-EXPERIAN (888-397-3742)
www.experian.com
Experian requires consumers who have found inaccuracies in their credit reports to file their disputes online. For details, go to **www.experian.com/disputes/index.html.**

TransUnion Consumer Solutions
P.O. Box 2000
Chester, PA 19022-2000
(800) 916-8800
www.transunion.com
You can download a dispute form at **www.transunion.com/docs/personal/InvestigationRequest_Chester.pdf.**
You can file a dispute online at **http://annualcreditreport.transunion.com/entry/disputeonline.**

YOUR CREDIT SCORE NUMBER
REALLY DOES MATTER

Even in the best of times, your credit score deeply impacts your ability to get out of debt and stay out of debt. The worse your credit score, the higher the interest rate you will be charged on money you borrow—if you can get a loan at all. The better your score, the less your debt will cost you—and the quicker you'll be able to pay it off.

I've been talking about the importance of knowing your credit score now for at least a decade. But the truth is that it's never been as important as it is today. As I said earlier, your credit score not only impacts your ability to borrow money, it can also affect your ability to get a job or even keep a job. Employers now routinely check the credit scores of prospective employees. Indeed, I hear every week from people who tell me they think they didn't get a job because of their credit score. People are also losing promotions due to bad credit scores. I recently had the privilege of giving a series of speeches at the Pentagon, and the military leaders there told me that they take credit scores so seriously that a bad one can actually prevent a soldier from being promoted. (That's because they consider someone with bad credit to be a security risk.)

JUST LIKE YOUR FINANCES,
YOUR CREDIT SCORE CHANGES ALL THE TIME

Much like your grade point average (or GPA) in school, your credit score is a measure of your ability—in this case, your ability to handle credit (otherwise known as your creditworthiness). A good score means you are a safe person to lend money to; a bad one means you may be too risky. Lenders use your score to decide whether they should loan you money and, if so, how much interest they should charge you.

Maybe you were told your credit score when you bought a car or refinanced your house a few years back. Well, don't assume it's still the same today. Your score is based on a variety of factors, all of which reflect some aspect of your financial behavior—how much you borrow, whether or not you pay your bills on time, etc. The result is a three-digit number that is constantly updated, depending on how and what you're doing financially. Indeed, in the summer of 2010, FICO announced that the number of people with a score below 600—meaning lenders will regard them as poor risks—had jumped by about 2.4 million over the previous two years.

This increase, which was obviously the result of the recession, brought the total number of Americans with poor credit to more than 43 million—or just over 25% of all consumers. Given that historically only around 15% of consumers scored below 600, this represented a huge change. And since scoring below 600 means that you probably won't be able to get credit cards, auto loans, or mortgages under the tighter lending standards banks now use, it highlights the importance of making sure you know what your score is right now.

So even if you pulled your score six months ago, you should pull it again today. And don't worry that pulling your score will affect your rating. Checking on yourself is considered a "soft inquiry," which you are allowed to do as much as you want—as opposed to a hard inquiry from a potential lender, too many of which can hurt your score.

IN TRUTH, YOU HAVE
MORE THAN ONE CREDIT SCORE

While everyone says you should check your credit score, what you should be checking are your *scores*. In fact, you have more than one. That's because lenders, creditors, and the three national credit-reporting agencies—Equifax, Experian, and TransUnion—all have their own particular methods and formulas for calculating what kind of a credit risk you are. They may also have different information about you.

The most widely used rating is the FICO score. Many people think the term "FICO score" is just another way of saying credit score (sort of the way people call all adhesive bandages Band-Aids and all facial tissues Kleenex). It's not. While FICO is the oldest and most popular credit-scoring system, the Big Three credit-reporting agencies have their own rating system (Equifax, Experian, and TransUnion).

That said, the credit-reporting agencies all base their individual scoring systems on mathematical models developed by Fair Isaac. So while your FICO score may differ slightly from the scores calculated by the credit-rating agencies, it's not likely to be wildly different. In other words, if you have a great FICO score, chances are your credit score from the three credit bureaus will be pretty good too. The opposite is also true: bad FICO score, bad score from the bureaus.

YOU'VE GOT YOUR REPORT—
NOW FIND OUT YOUR SCORE

As I mentioned before, your credit report is not your credit score. Your score is *based* on your reports—and, unfortunately, while the law gives you free access to your credit report, you have to pay extra to get the score. The simplest route to get your real credit score is to buy it. You can buy it right now from Fair Isaac and the three credit bureaus. As of this writing, the average cost is $15.95.

WHERE TO BUY YOUR CREDIT SCORE

www.myfico.com (its score is called the FICO Score)
www.equifax.com (its score is called the Equifax Credit Score)
www.experian.com (its score is called the PLUS Score)
www.transunion.com (its score is called the VantageScore)

GET YOUR FREE CREDIT SCORE AT
WWW.FINISHRICH.COM

As I mentioned earlier, purchasers of this book can get their credit score from Equifax FOR FREE. So I suggest that you head to my website at **www.finishrich.com/debtwise** and take advantage of the free DebtWise.com trial, which has a value of $14.95. By signing up, you will be entitled to a free Equifax Credit Score.

There are many websites around these days that claim to offer free credit scores (usually called a "Credit Report Card" or some similar name). But more often than not, most sites currently offering "free credit scores" don't really give you your real credit score. Rather, they provide a simulation—and then sell your contact information to online marketers of credit-monitoring services. If you don't want the spam that comes with this, read the small print or the FAQ section of the website before you sign up. Also, if you ever sign up for a "free credit score," be sure to read the agreement carefully to see if you will automatically be charged a monthly membership fee after the 30-day trial period. Most websites that offer "free" credit scores charge you once the free trial period ends and offer a "credit-monitoring service" with membership. I think having a credit-monitoring service can be worth it, but you should know what you are signing up for before you sign. So read the fine print of any site that says "FREE." (By the way, keep in mind that DebtWise.com is also a membership site, and the offer included in this book is for just one month free. After that, there is a monthly membership fee. So, again, read the fine print before you sign up!)

WHAT GOES INTO YOUR CREDIT SCORE— AND WHAT COMES OUT

So how do the credit-rating companies decide what score to assign you? What they do is take your credit history based on your credit reports and run it through a complicated series of calculations. In the case of FICO, the result is a number somewhere between 300 and 850. This is your FICO score. Anything over 720 is considered good. Score 740 or higher and most lenders will give you their best deals. On the other hand, a score below 600 means you will have trouble getting a loan no matter how high an interest rate you're willing to pay. Fannie Mae, the giant mortgage-buying agency, will not consider guaranteeing a mortgage unless the borrower has a FICO score of at least 620.

On its website, Fair Isaac spells out how it weighs the various factors that go into calculating your score. They are, in order of importance:

- **35% of Your Score: Payment History.** Do you always pay your bills on time or do you have delinquencies? Any bankruptcies, liens, judgments, garnishments, etc., on your record? PAY ATTENTION TO THIS! Simply paying your bills on time impacts more than a third of your score.

- **30%: Amounts Owed.** How much do you owe? What kinds of debt do you have? What proportion of your total credit limit is being used? Most experts agree that a credit utilization of more than 30% will hurt your score. So if your Visa card has a credit limit of, say, $5,000, you'll want to avoid carrying a balance of more than $1,500 at any one time. According to FICO, more than half of all credit card users manage to do this. On the other hand, one in seven are using more than 80% of their available credit.

- **15%: Length of Credit History.** How long since you opened your first credit account? How old is your oldest active account? (The average is 14 years; the longer your history, the better.) This is why you should no longer close old accounts you don't use—and why when you are asked to "opt out" now by credit card companies you should still keep the accounts open even after you have paid them off.

- **10%: New Credit.** How many accounts have you opened recently? How many recent inquiries by potential lenders? A lot of new activity makes the credit-rating agencies nervous.

- **10%: Types of Credit Used.** How many different kinds of active credit accounts do you have? A varied mix of credit—e.g., credit cards, installment loans, mortgages, retail accounts, etc.—is a plus; too much of one type is a minus. According to FICO, the average consumer has 13 active credit accounts at any given time—nine of them for credit cards and four for installment loans.

FICO and the other companies keep the details of their scoring formulas top-secret. But they are very open about the fact that they are designed to ring alarm bells at the first sign that you're getting in over your head. In 2009, the personal-finance columnist Liz Pulliam Weston persuaded FICO to explain exactly how certain actions affect its scoring. The results are worth studying. For example, it turns out that maxing out a credit card can knock anywhere from 10 to 45 points off your credit score—even if you pay off the balance in full right away. Skipping a payment cycle (that is, being more than 30 days late with the minimum payment) can cost you 60 to 110 points. And debt settlements—which happen when you take advantage of one of those programs that promise to "settle your debts for just pennies on the dollar"—will reduce your score by 45 to 125 points. (By the way, getting out of an underwater mortgage by arranging what's called a "short sale"— in which you sell your house for less than you owe and your lender writes off the remaining balance—is generally reported as a settlement.)

Not surprisingly, the real credit-score killers are foreclosure and bankruptcy. Having your mortgage foreclosed will slash your credit score by 85 to 160 points, while declaring bankruptcy can shrink your score by as much as a third, cutting anywhere from 130 to 240 points in one fell swoop. No wonder an FTC official once called bankruptcy the nuclear bomb of credit actions.

RAISING YOUR SCORE BY 100 POINTS
CAN SAVE YOU $100,000

Fair Isaac claims that the median FICO score in the United States is around 720—meaning that half of all Americans score higher than that and half score lower. But they've been saying that since 2005, and many experts think the real figure is much lower. According to Experian, the average U.S. credit score is 693.

This may not seem like much of a discrepancy. But it is. It's amazing how dramatically a difference of just 50 to 100 points on your FICO score can change everything when it comes to borrowing money. The table below shows how differing credit scores will affect the mortgage rates banks are willing to offer you.

HOW YOUR CREDIT SCORE AFFECTS YOUR MORTGAGE (based on a $300,000, 30-year fixed-rate mortgage)		
Score	Interest Rate	Monthly Payment
760-850	4.650%	$1,547
700-759	4.872%	$1,587
680-699	5.049%	$1,619
660-679	5.263%	$1,659
640-659	5.693%	$1,740
620-639	6.239%	$1,845
Source: Fair Isaac; May 6, 2010		

Among other things, what this table shows is that a person with a credit score of 630 would have to pay $1,845 a month for a $300,000 30-year fixed-rate mortgage, while the monthly payment for someone with a 760 score would be just $1,547. You don't think that's such a big deal? Think again.

Say you're the person with the 630 score. If you could raise it by 130 points—which, as you will see in a minute, you can easily do—you could probably refinance and wind up with a monthly mortgage payment that's roughly $300 less than what you're paying now. Let's say that instead of spending that extra $300 on something else, you added it to your mortgage payment. In other words, you continued to pay the same monthly amount as before, but now $300 more is going to principal instead of interest. Can you guess what this would do to your ability to pay off your mortgage? Instead of taking you 30 years to pay it off, you'd be debt free in less than 21 years—and your total interest bill would be reduced by a whopping $126,945.

This is just one example of how improving your credit score can help you get out of debt. So let's get going!

DEBT FREE FOR LIFE SUCCESS STORY

David, I did exactly what you suggested in your book *Start Over, Finish Rich*—and sure enough, in less than a year I have been able to raise my credit score over 60 points. By paying down my debt, always paying on time, and fixing mistakes on my credit report files, my score has gone from 680 to over 740. Thanks to the higher score I've been able to refinance my home and lock in a 30-year mortgage at 4.25%! I will save over $41,000 in interest because of the refinance. Thank you so much for all you do, and all you share.

Richard S.
Long Island, New York

A 12-STEP ACTION PLAN
TO IMPROVE YOUR SCORE

The simple truth is that raising your score isn't that hard if you know what to do. It's mainly a matter of understanding the factors that FICO and the credit bureaus weigh and then figuring out which of them you can change for the better. As I said before, I've coached literally thousands of people on fixing their credit scores, and based on that experience I've developed a 12-step action plan to get your score up quickly and keep it there. I promise you—regardless of where you are starting from, if you follow this plan, in six months your score will be higher than you thought possible.

> **STEP NO. 1**
> **Get your credit report and check it for errors.**

I explained before how common mistakes are in credit reports and how easy it is to get them corrected. Once you get your report from **www.annualcreditreport.com,** go through it with a fine-tooth comb and bring any damaging errors you may find (for example, late payments that were actually paid on time or credit limits that are lower than they should be) to the attention of the credit agency by sending them a certified letter. Remember, under the Fair Credit Reporting Act, the credit-reporting agencies are required to correct inaccurate or incomplete information in your report within 30 days after it's pointed out to them. (Occasionally, errors can help you, as when accounts you closed are listed as being open; don't feel obliged to correct these.)

> ### STEP NO. 2
> ### Automate your bill-paying
> ### so you never miss a deadline.

This may be the most important tip. Missing payments—even just one—can really hurt your credit score. For this reason, I strongly recommend that you use your bank's online bill-paying service to automatically transfer a pre-set amount every month from your checking account to cover at least the minimum payments on all your credit accounts. I personally have every single bill of mine "automated" in this way. As a result, I never need to worry about being late on any payment, even if I am traveling.

> ### STEP NO. 3
> ### If you have missed payments,
> ### get on it and get current.

It's never too late to clean up your act. Get yourself current as quickly as you can and then stay current. Your score will begin to improve within a few months—and the longer you keep it up, the more noticeable the increase will be. The negative weight FICO gives to bad behavior like delinquencies lessens over time, so as long as you stay on the straight and narrow, those black marks will eventually disappear from your record for good. But remember—late payments can stay on your record for up to seven years—so get those bills paid on time. The sooner you get a record of paying at least the minimums, the better.

> ### STEP NO. 4
> ## Keep your balance well below your credit limit.

Of all the factors you can control—and improve quickly—how much you owe is probably the most powerful. What makes this especially important is that ever since the credit crunch first hit in the fall of 2008, credit card companies have been cutting customers' credit limits without warning. According to one banking analyst, the amount of credit available to consumers through credit cards and other credit lines has been cut in half in recent years—from a total of $5 trillion at the beginning of 2008 to just $2.5 trillion at the end of 2010. On a personal basis, this can be devastating to your credit score. Say you've got a $1,000 balance on a card with a $2,000 credit limit—and then the card company slashes your limit to $1,000. Suddenly, you've gone from 50% credit utilization to being maxed out, which can shave 45 points from your credit score. The credit bureaus recommend that you keep your usage below 33% of your available credit. Since there's nothing you can do to protect your score if a credit card company reduces your limit arbitrarily, it's vitally important to keep your credit utilization as low as possible at all times.

> ### STEP NO. 5
> ## Beware of the credit card transfer game.

For years, people have been saving money by transferring high-interest credit card balances to low-interest cards. This can still be helpful, but be aware that using one credit line to pay off another sets off credit-score alarm bells—even if all you're doing is consolidating your accounts. All other things being equal, your credit score will be higher if you have a bunch of small balances on a number of different cards rather than a big balance on just one or two.

STEP NO. 6
If you rack up high balances, pay your credit card bill *early*.

The "Amounts Owed" part of your credit score is based on the balance due listed on your most recent credit card statements. So even if you pay your bills in full each month, running up high balances can still hurt your score. You can avoid this problem by paying down all or part of your bill *before* the end of your statement period, thus reducing the balance due that will be reported to FICO and the credit bureaus.

STEP NO. 7
Hang on to your old accounts, even if you're not using them.

Part of your credit score is based on how long you have had credit accounts. Closing old accounts shortens your credit history and reduces your total credit—neither of which is good for your credit score. If you have to close an account, close a relatively new one and keep the older ones open. Also, ***closing an account will not remove a bad payment record from your report.*** Closed accounts are listed right along with active ones.

STEP NO. 8
Use your old cards.

In the aftermath of the credit crunch, the credit card industry has gotten much more strict about closing inactive accounts.

This can hurt your credit score, since it reduces the average age of your credit accounts. To prevent this from happening to you, pull out your old cards and start putting at least one charge on each of them every month. This will keep the account open, which in turn will keep your credit history nice and long—and ultimately raise your score.

STEP NO. 9
Demonstrate that you can be responsible.

The best way to raise your score is to demonstrate that you can handle credit responsibly—which means not borrowing too much and paying back what you do borrow on time. Don't open new accounts just to increase your available credit or create a better variety of credit. This is especially true if you are just beginning to establish a credit history. Adding a lot of new accounts may look risky—and it will definitely lower the average age of your accounts, which can hurt your score if you don't have much of a track record. You should open new credit accounts only if and when you need them.

STEP NO. 10
When you're shopping for a loan, do it quickly.

When you apply for a loan, the lender will "run your credit"— that is, send an inquiry to one of the credit-rating agencies to find out how creditworthy you are. Too many such inquiries can hurt your FICO score, since that could indicate you're trying to borrow money from many different sources. Of course, you can generate a lot of inquiries doing something perfectly reasonable—like shopping for the best mortgage or auto loan by applying to a number of different lenders. The FICO scoring system is designed to allow for this by considering the length of time over which a series of inquiries are made. So try to do all your loan shopping within 30 days, so the inquiries get batched together and it's obvious to FICO that you are loan shopping.

STEP NO. 11

Know the difference between a "soft inquiry" and a "hard inquiry."

Fair Isaac and the credit bureaus all recognize the difference between you checking your own score (what is called a "soft inquiry") and the banks or lending organizations checking your score (a "hard inquiry"). While too many hard inquiries can lower your score, soft inquiries don't count against you at all. So feel free to check your credit score as often as you want.

STEP NO. 12

Consider buying a 3-and-1 Report as well as a credit-monitoring package and identity-theft service.

I am constantly urging my readers not to sign up for unnecessary monthly expenses. That said, I really do think that your credit score and your credit report are so important that it makes sense to pay for a 3-and-1 Report (which provides you with your credit scores from the three big bureaus) as well as an identity-theft monitoring service. Any of the three credit bureaus will sell you a 3-and-1 Report for roughly the same price. And all of them now offer Identity Theft Monitoring Programs. In most cases, these services will cost you between $14.95 and $19.95 a month, depending on the company. I personally pay for this kind of service myself because I think it's worth the investment.

Congratulations! You now know more than 95% of all Americans about what may well be the most important influence over your financial life—your credit record and score. Now let's look at how to handle what is probably the biggest single debt you will ever have.

DEBT FREE FOR LIFE ACTION STEPS

❏ Go to **www.annualcreditreport.com** and pull your credit reports from all three major credit bureaus.

❏ Check the reports for errors and if you find any, request a correction immediately.

❏ Pull your credit score FOR FREE from **www.finishrich. com.**

❏ Follow the 12-step plan to improve your score.

CHAPTER NINE

MORTGAGE DEBT:
HOW TO PROTECT YOUR HOME AND
PAY OFF YOUR MORTGAGE EARLY

If you're a homeowner, your mortgage is almost certainly the biggest single debt you have—or ever will have. In fact, your mortgage is probably several times bigger than all your other debts put together. As I write this in the summer of 2010, the latest Federal Reserve statistics show that Americans owe a total of $10.7 trillion in home mortgage debt—compared to just $2.4 trillion in auto loans, credit card balances, and every other kind of consumer debt.

So if you're going to be debt free for life, the place to start is figuring out how to pay off your mortgage as quickly as possible. And that's what this chapter is about. In the pages that follow, I'm going to share with you my foolproof plan to pay any mortgage off years early—and save tens of thousands of dollars or more in interest payments.

I'll also show you how to make sure you have the right kind of mortgage, what to do if you don't, and then finally what to do if you are having trouble making your payments. The fact is, for many of us these days, the issue isn't how fast we can pay off our mortgage, but whether we can pay it off at all. The good news is that there are a variety of programs designed to make your mortgage more affordable. By the time we're finished here, you'll know exactly whom to call and where to go to get your interest rate lowered and maybe even your principal amount reduced.

PAY OFF YOUR MORTGAGE EARLY—
AND SAVE HUNDREDS OF THOUSANDS
OF DOLLARS IN THE PROCESS

For homeowners, the key to becoming debt free for life is paying off your mortgage as quickly as possible. Of course you can't even think about doing that unless you have the right kind of mortgage—which is to say, a 15- or 30-year fixed mortgage with payments you can afford to make. Later on in this chapter, I'll explain what you should do if you don't have the right mortgage. But for the moment, let's assume you do. How do you pay it off as quickly as possible?

Well, if you can manage the higher monthly payments, there is no question that signing up for a 15-year fixed mortgage is the way to go. Not only will you be free of your mortgage debt sooner, but you will also save a lot of money in the process. And when I say a lot, I mean A LOT.

Let's say you have a $300,000 mortgage with a 6% interest rate. As the following table shows, paying it off in 15 years instead of 30 would reduce the total cost of the loan by nearly a third—a savings to you of roughly *$192,000!* Of course, your monthly payments would be $733 higher with the shorter term ($2,532 a month vs. $1,799 a month), but if you can manage to write the bigger check, it will pay off for you big-time over the long run. Just think what you could do with an extra $192,000. This is definitely a case where a little short-term pain equals a huge long-term gain.

Many of you are worried about the stock market and whether or not you can trust it. The one investment you can definitely trust is debt reduction—which is why paying down your mortgage is such a smart investment in an uncertain world.

	15-year mortgage	30-year mortgage
COST OF A 15-YEAR AND A 30-YEAR FIXED MORTGAGE Amount: $300,000 Annual Interest: 6.00%		
Monthly payment	$2,532	$1,799
Total interest	$155,683	$347,515
Total payments	$455,683	$647,515
SOURCE: Bankrate.com		

WHAT IF A 15-YEAR MORTGAGE IS JUST TOO EXPENSIVE FOR YOU?

I know that, especially these days, most people simply can't afford to make the higher monthly payments that go along with a 15-year fixed mortgage. But that doesn't mean there's nothing you can do to speed up the day when your home will be debt free.

In my previous books, I've described a simple system that any homeowner can use to pay off a 30-year mortgage as much as seven years early. When people hear about it, they often think it's a trick.

It's not.

Think about it this way. The problem with a 30-year mortgage is that it's designed to make you spend 30 years paying it off! Let's stick with our example of a $300,000 mortgage at 6%. If you take the full 30 years to pay it off, you will wind up actually giving the bank close to $648,000, since in addition to paying back the principal, you will make nearly $348,000 in interest payments.

Here's a better approach. What if you were to take that same mortgage and make the payments on a biweekly instead of a monthly schedule? I know it's hard to believe, but this simple change can cut the total payment time by six years—and in the process save you $72,000 in interest payments.

PAY YOUR MORTGAGE FASTER— PAINLESSLY

Here's how it works. All you do is take the normal 30-year mortgage you have and instead of making the monthly payment the way you normally do, you split it down the middle and pay half every two weeks.

Say your mortgage payment is $1,800 a month (which is what it is in the example we just used). Under my biweekly plan, instead of sending a $1,800 check to your mortgage lender once every month, you would send him $900 every two weeks. At the beginning, paying $900 every two weeks probably won't feel any different from paying $1,800 once a month. But as anyone who's ever looked at a calendar could tell you, it's not really the same thing. A month, after all, is a little longer than four weeks. And so what happens as a result of switching to a biweekly payment plan is that over the course of a year you gradually get further and further ahead in your payments, until by the end of the year you have paid the equivalent of not 12 but 13 monthly payments. Best of all, because it is so gradual, you will hardly feel the pinch.

The math is actually quite simple. A monthly mortgage payment of $1,800 amounts to $21,600 a year. But when you make a half payment every two weeks instead of a full one once a month, you end up making 26 half payments over the course of a year. That's 26 payments of $900—for a total of $23,400, or one extra month's worth of payments, painlessly.

> ### DEBT FREE FOR LIFE SUCCESS STORY
>
> Taking your advice on paying down principal early, I have set up my mortgage payments automatically and I submit two full extra payments per year. At this rate, my home will be paid off in twelve years versus thirty and I will have saved tens of thousands of dollars in interest—not to mention that the house (now a rental) is bringing in positive cash flow. I will be financially comfortable by age 43, with all the leisure time in the world to enjoy life and pursue other business and investment opportunities. Best of all, I will have NO mortgage. Thanks again!
>
> **Marc B.**
> **San Diego, CA**

WHAT COULD YOU DO WITH AN EXTRA $72,000?

The impact of that extra month's payment is awesome. Depending on your interest rate, you will end up paying off a 30-year mortgage somewhere between five and seven years early, and a 15-year mortgage three years early! You will be debt free years ahead of schedule, saving you tens of thousands of dollars in interest payments over the life of your loan.

I'm not just making these figures up. Check out the amortization schedule on the next page. It shows the difference between a monthly and a biweekly payment plan for a $300,000, 30-year mortgage with an interest rate of 6%. The monthly pay-off schedule winds up incurring a total of $347,515 in interest charges over the life of the loan. The biweekly schedule, on the other hand, runs up just $275,100 in interest. In other words, switching to the biweekly plan will save you more than $72,000.

MONTHLY PAYMENTS VS. BIWEEKLY PAYMENTS		
Principal = $300,000 Interest Rate = 6.00 % Term = 30 years		
Monthly Payment: $1,798.65		Biweekly Payment: $899.33
Total Interest: $347,515		Total Interest: $275,100
Year	Principal Balance (Monthly Payments)	Principal Balance (Biweekly Payments)
1	$300,000.00	$294,490.01
2	$296,316.00	$288,640.16
3	$292,404.74	$282,429.52
4	$288,252.26	$275,835.82
5	$283,843.65	$268,835.44
6	$279,163.14	$261,403.29
7	$274,193.95	$253,512.75
8	$268,918.26	$245,135.52
9	$263,317.20	$236,241.60
10	$257,370.66	$226,799.14
11	$251,057.36	$216,774.28
12	$244,354.68	$206,131.11
13	$237,238.59	$194,831.49
14	$229,683.57	$182,834.92
15	$221,662.63	$170,098.43

16	$213,146.93	$156,576.40
17	$204,106.01	$142,220.34
18	$194,507.47	$126,978.85
19	$184,316.92	$110,797.29
20	$173,497.81	$93,617.70
21	$162,011.42	$75,378.51
22	$149,816.56	$56,014.35
23	$136,869.55	$35,455.85
24	$123,124.02	$13,629.36
25	$108,530.68	$0.00
26	$93,037.25	$0.00
27	$76,588.22	$0.00
28	$59,124.65	$0.00
29	$40,583.98	$0.00
30	$20,899.75	$0.00
Result:	Paid off in 30 years	Paid off in 24 years
SOURCE: Bankrate.com "Biweekly mortgage payment calculator"		

If you'd like to figure out how much you could save on your own mortgage, go online and visit my website at **www. finishrich.com**. First, click on "Learn," then look under "Free Resources" and click the "Get a biweekly mortgage payment plan" Calculator. This will take you to the best free calculator I've found on the Internet. You can then plug in your own numbers and quickly see how much you could save by switching to a biweekly payment plan.

ALL IT TAKES IS FIVE MINUTES

The great thing about switching to a biweekly payment plan is that it allows you to save money over the long run without refinancing or otherwise changing your mortgage. All it takes is one call.

That's because these days most mortgage lenders offer programs designed to totally automate the process I've just described.

To enroll, all you need to do is phone your lender or go online to its website. And many banks offer this service for free to customers who do all their banking with them. Those that don't usually refer you to an outside company that runs the program for them. These companies generally charge a set-up fee of between $200 and $400. In addition, there's a transfer charge of $2.50 to $6.95 that's assessed every time your money is moved from your checking account to your mortgage account.

A lot of companies now provide these services. To be sure you're dealing with a reputable firm, you should probably use one that is referred to you by your bank.

WHY NOT DO IT YOURSELF?

Why spend hundreds of dollars on an outside firm when you could just as easily use your bank's online automatic bill-paying service to schedule biweekly mortgage payments for yourself? Unfortunately it's not really that simple.

The problem is that if you split your monthly mortgage payment in half and send it in to your mortgage lender every two weeks yourself, the lender will simply send it back to you because they won't know what to do with it. Or worse, they'll stick the money in an escrow account and just let it sit there. Believe it or not, standard operating procedure at many banks is to take extra payments and hold them in a non-interest-bearing account—not use them to pay down your mortgage.

WHAT YOU COULD DO FOR FREE

You could add 10% to your regular mortgage check each month and have the money applied toward the principal. Or you could make one extra payment at the end of the year and again have it go toward your principal. But note that word "could." Let's face it—some things are much easier said than done.

If you decide to do it yourself, my suggestion is that you add an extra 10% a month toward your mortgage payment—*and make the payment automatic.* (To learn how to make it automatic, see Chapter Fifteen.) Also, make a point of asking your bank to make sure that this extra payment is credited toward your principal—and then check your monthly statements to make sure they did it correctly.

PENNY-WISE OR POUND-FOOLISH?

Some people are put off by the cost of a biweekly payment. But think about it. When all is said and done, running a biweekly payment plan shouldn't cost you more than $100 a year. For this modest expense (less than $2,500 over the life of the loan), you will save tens of thousands of dollars. In the example I provided earlier, the savings totaled more than

$72,000. Some readers have told me this one idea saved them more than twice that!

And a biweekly payment plan does more than allow you to pay off your home early. It also makes it easier to manage your money, since most of us get paid every two weeks. You'll be richer faster, with a plan that makes your life easier. As I say, it's a key part of being debt free for life.

FROM BOOM TO BUST:
THE HOMEOWNER'S NIGHTMARE

As I write this in the summer of 2010, we're just coming off of a scary four-year roller-coaster ride in which real estate values dropped nationally by around 30%—and in some parts of the country by a lot more than that. The good news is that home prices finally seem to have bottomed out. The bad news is that as of the beginning of 2010, some 11 million U.S. homeowners—or one out of five—were "under water," owing more on their mortgages than their houses were worth. With unemployment still a huge problem, more than 7 million homeowners were having trouble making their payments. Nearly 2 million families had already lost their homes to foreclosure in the previous two years—and economists were predicting that over the next five years, another 8 million to 13 million Americans would likely suffer a similar fate.

So even though home prices have probably stopped falling, few experts expect a big rebound in real estate values any time soon.

Those who have read my other books know that I've always been a great advocate of homeownership. Nothing you do in your lifetime is likely to make you as much money as buying a home and living in it. Despite the pain and turmoil of the last few years, I still believe this. As I see it, the most important real estate lesson we can draw from what we've been through is simply that there are no shortcuts to successful homeownership. There are two rules in particular that you should always follow: (1) always make sure you have the right kind of mortgage; and (2) never borrow more than you can afford to pay back. In other words, never buy a home that you can't comfortably afford.

WHAT DO YOU DO IF YOU DON'T HAVE THE RIGHT KIND OF MORTGAGE?

As I said at the beginning of this chapter, my early pay-off plan won't work unless you have the right kind of mortgage— a 15- or 30-year fixed mortgage with payments you can afford. There are no surprises with a 30-year fixed: You know exactly what your payments are going to be for the life of the mortgage and you pay down principal with every payment, reducing the amount you owe and building equity every month.

So my recommendation is that if you plan to be in your home more than five years and you have anything but a 15- or 30-year fixed mortgage—say, one of those adjustable-rate deals that have gotten so many people in trouble—then you should refinance NOW. Rates are at historic lows as I write this—but this won't last forever.

The best place to start mortgage shopping is online. First, go to a website like **www.lendingtree.com, www.quickenloans. com** or **www.bankrate.com** and see what mortgage lenders are offering. Then call your current lender and ask if he can match the best deal you found online.

WHAT YOU NEED TO KNOW ABOUT REFINANCING

Lending standards are much tighter than they used to be, but if you can meet the requirements, most banks will be happy to refinance your mortgage. The three basic criteria are:

- **Your debt-to-income ratio, or DTI.** Mortgage lenders want your DTI to be less than 38%. That is, your monthly mortgage payments shouldn't total more than 38% of your monthly income.

- **Your loan-to-value ratio, or LTV.** Most lenders want it to be less than 80%—meaning the total amount you owe on your house should be no more than 80% of what the house is worth. (For example, if your house is worth $200,000, they will not refinance a mortgage of more than $160,000.)

- **Your credit score.** As I noted in Chapter Eight, you'll generally need a FICO score of at least 620 to even be considered for a loan—and at least 740 to get the best interest rates.

When you compare mortgages, you will need to take note of the annual percentage rate (APR), whether the lender is charging you "points" up front (you don't want this), and what the closing costs will be (including fees for appraisals, title search, title insurance, credit reports, etc.). Refinancing only makes sense if the savings you enjoy from lower interest payments more than cover the cost of closing the new mortgage. If you are going to be in your home for more than another three years, you'll generally come out ahead as long as your new interest rate is at least one full percentage point lower than what you are currently paying. Have your bank run a "break-even analysis" for you. They can do this in a matter of minutes and tell you, "Yup, the cost of refinancing will be paid off in 28 months [or whatever]." You need to know this before you pull the trigger on your "refi."

WHAT DO YOU DO IF YOU CAN'T AFFORD TO MAKE YOUR MORTGAGE PAYMENTS?

The worry of losing your home can be paralyzing—but when you are faced with foreclosure, doing nothing is the biggest mistake you can make.

With this in mind, if you have a mortgage you can no longer afford and are unable to refinance, I want you to go online NOW and visit the federal government's "Making Home Affordable" website at **www.makinghomeaffordable.gov.**

Making Home Affordable was introduced with great fanfare early in 2009 by the Obama Administration. It was billed at the time as an attempt to help as many as 9 million struggling homeowners by reducing their monthly mortgage payments to more affordable levels. Making Home Affordable offered two different potential solutions for borrowers: (1) the Home Affordable Refinance Program (HARP), which gives homeowners with Fannie Mae or Freddie Mac mortgages an opportunity to refinance into more affordable monthly payments; and (2) the Home Affordable Modification Program (HAMP), which committed $75 billion to keep people in their homes by preventing avoidable foreclosures.

As of this writing in the middle of 2010, HARP has done a pretty good job, refinancing more than 4 million Fannie Mae and Freddie Mac loans. HAMP, on the other hand, has been something of a disappointment. The hope was that by the end of 2012 it would give up to 4 million homeowners some breathing room by reducing their mortgage rates to as low as 2% for five years and extending loan terms to as long as 40 years—thus lowering their monthly payments. Unfortunately, that's not how it worked out. By the middle of 2010, only 340,000 homeowners—or just 27% of the 1.2 million who signed up for HAMP in its first 16 months—had managed to get their mortgages permanently modified.

AN EXPANDED PROGRAM TO HELP MORE PEOPLE

The problem was that when HAMP was originally put together, no one expected the recession to last so long or unemployment to stay so high. HAMP was meant to deal mainly with subprime borrowers who should never have bought a home in the first place, not millions of longtime homeowners who were suddenly facing foreclosure because they had lost their jobs in the worst economic downturn since the Great Depression. Most of these people had so many debts in addition to their home loans that even with mortgage modifications that lowered their monthly payments, they still couldn't afford to make them and as a result had to drop out of the program.

In an effort to solve the problem, the White House has expanded HAMP, making it more flexible and adding provisions specifically meant to help unemployed homeowners. Along these lines, the government also introduced a new program called the Home Affordable Unemployment Program (HAUP), under which jobless homeowners can get a "forbearance"—meaning their monthly mortgage payments get reduced or even suspended entirely for at least three months.

TO QUALIFY, YOU NEED TO BE IN TROUBLE

The easiest way to determine if you qualify for HARP, HAMP, or any of the other mortgage relief programs the government offers is to go to the "Making Home Affordable" website (**www.makinghomeaffordable.gov**), click on "Eligibility," and complete the brief self-assessment checklist for the program you're interested in. While this tool will help you determine if you are eligible, only the servicer of your loan can say for sure, so you must contact them for more information. If you are behind on your mortgage payments, you probably won't qualify for HARP. However, you may qualify for HAMP or, if you're out of work, HAUP.

Basically, to be eligible to have your mortgage modified under the Making Home Affordable program, your mortgage servicer has to be participating in the program and you need to be in trouble. Specifically, you must have a "front end" debt-to-income ratio greater than 31%. That is, the total of your monthly mortgage principal, interest, taxes, insurance, and homeowner's association dues must be more than 31% of your gross household income. In fact, according to the Treasury Department, the median DTI ratio of homeowners who get Making Home Affordable mortgage modifications is 44.8%. (If your income is too high for the program, you can ask your lender to work with you directly. Unfortunately, unless you're in default or close to it—meaning you've missed three consecutive payments—most lenders can't be bothered.)

Your lender should provide you with the forms you need to apply for a Making Home Affordable mortgage modification. Fill them out carefully and make sure you include ALL the requested documents. (These usually include your most recent mortgage statement, your pay stubs for the previous two months, at least two consecutive checking-account statements, your latest tax return, an itemized list of your expenses, your utility bills for the most recent month, and a "hardship" letter explaining why you need help.) The government kicks back lots of applications to the banks unapproved. As an official of the Mortgage Bankers Association told the *Los Angeles Times,* in 99% of these cases it's because the packages are either missing documents or contain mistakes.

Once you've filled out your forms and sent them in, it takes about 60 days for everything to be processed. But don't just sit back and wait. Forms get lost and paperwork gets misfiled all the time, so call your bank every two weeks to check on the status of your application.

WHAT TO DO IF YOUR LENDER WON'T HELP YOU

If you're not getting the help you need from your lender or mortgage servicer, talk to a housing counselor approved by the U.S. Department of Housing and Urban Development (HUD). He or she will help you navigate the process—free of charge. For a referral, visit the HUD website at **www.hud. gov** or call toll-free (800) 569-4287. Remember, the earlier you get help, the more options you will have and the better your chances will be to save your home.

REMEMBER, YOU HAVE TO LIVE SOMEWHERE

My last words of advice regarding your home and your mortgage is to keep in mind that you have to live somewhere. The beauty of owning your own home is that if you pay down your mortgage, the cost of homeownership will eventually be cheaper than renting. One of the biggest mistakes homeowners made during the housing bubble was to treat their homes like they were ATM machines, continually drawing on their home-equity lines of credit to pay for consumer goods—and pay off credit card debt.

It's time now to go back to the basics of homeownership, where you buy less house than you can afford and pay off your home faster. I noted earlier that as of this writing, mortgages are being refinanced at a record pace, and about a third of these deals involve homeowners putting money into their homes, not taking it out. We are also seeing a record number of 30-year mortgages being refinanced into 15-year mortgages. All of this will help the real estate markets stabilize eventually, and ultimately we will see home prices begin to appreciate again. But for you, right now and forever, the key is to focus on paying down your debt. A debt-free home is a really nice home to live in—and it's absolutely worth striving for!

DEBT FREE FOR LIFE ACTION STEPS

❏ Use the mortgage calculators at **www.finishrich.com** to see how much more quickly you could pay off your mortgage—and how much you could save—by switching to a biweekly payment plan.
❏ If you don't have a 30-year fixed mortgage with payments you can afford, ask your lender for a better deal and start shopping around online.
❏ If you can't afford your mortgage and are unable to refinance, check out the government's mortgage-relief programs at **www.makinghomeaffordable.gov.**

CHAPTER TEN

THE STUDENT LOAN DIET:
NINE GREAT WAYS TO CRUSH YOUR STUDENT DEBT AND SLEEP WELL AT NIGHT

This chapter is for anyone who has taken out student loans to pay for his or her education. It's also for anyone who may be considering borrowing money for college in the future.

Over the last two years, I have received more questions about student loans than I got in the previous two decades combined. The reason is brutally simple: Not only is college more expensive than ever (which makes borrowing harder to avoid), but because of the recession, it's also the hardest time in decades for college graduates to find decent employment—and thus earn the money they need to be able to pay off their loans.

This financial double-whammy is crushing a generation of young people under a mountain of debt many find impossible to manage. According to the most recent U.S. Department of Education statistics, two out of every three students who graduated from college in 2008 financed their education at least partly with student loans, with the typical borrower starting out his working life owing around $23,000. And since then, the problem has gotten worse, not better. In 2009, the total amount of federal student loans outstanding topped $605 billion. The private student loan market is a largely unregulated "wild west" market, making it more difficult to track, but experts figure it accounted for another $300 billion or so—which would have brought the grand total to somewhere close to $1 trillion.

This is a truly mind-blowing figure. And with this in mind, let's look at how you should borrow money for school—and ultimately get it paid off!

TIP NO. 1
Get the facts and understand the problem.

A generation ago, student loans were nearly unheard of. Now they're a nightmare!

Driven by college costs that are increasing at roughly twice the rate of inflation, borrowing for education has exploded to the point where student loans now represent about one-third of all non-real-estate consumer debt.

In the past I have argued that student loans are not only a good investment (because higher education generally leads to increased earnings potential) but also that they are a more intelligent form of debt than, say, a bank loan you might take out to buy a boat or car, or a credit card balance you run up to pay for a vacation. I have also pointed out repeatedly that student loans (particularly government-subsidized student loans) offer lower interest rates, meaning it's cheap money to borrow. And all of this is true. In recent years, however, I have begun to see some problems with student loans.

To begin with, people who borrow money for college often don't really understand what a serious commitment they are making. It's generally easier to get a student loan than it is to borrow money to buy a home or a car or get a credit card— and yet student loans are the most difficult loans to get out of if you get into financial trouble.

Another problem is that an increasing number of people are being forced to take out private student loans, which generally have variable interest rates (meaning they can get more expensive) and are virtually impossible to refinance.

And perhaps most troubling of all, the value of a higher education—the guarantee that a college degree will enable you to make more money—simply isn't as much of a "sure thing" as it used to be. When you borrow money for school, you're betting that you will be able to afford to pay back the loan after you graduate. But these days, with unemployment high, many college students wind up graduating into a world of no income—and lots of debt.

It's because of these factors that this chapter is so important to your Debt Free For Life Plan.

STUDENT LOANS ARE EASY TO GET AND HARD TO GET RID OF

Although I would never suggest you borrow money with the intention of not paying it back, the fact is that there are times when it's perfectly legal and proper to walk away from a debt. But that's never the case with student loans. It's important to understand that if you borrow money for college, you are going to be expected to pay it back come hell or high water! Short of paying it off in full, there is almost no way you can legally get out of this obligation. If you fall behind on your payments, your Social Security benefits can be garnished and you can be rendered ineligible for a security clearance and some government jobs. In most cases, not even bankruptcy can make it go away. And forget about trying to get excused because you're sick. According to the U.S. Department of Education, you can get your loans discharged for medical reasons only "in the event of total and permanent disability or death." If there's any possibility that you'll ever be able to earn an income doing anything ever again for the rest of your life, your student loans will not be discharged. No wonder Harvard Law

School professor and consumer advocate Elizabeth Warren once said that student loan collectors have powers that would "make a mobster envious."

Because of this, if you get overextended, your options will be pretty limited. Without the threat of bankruptcy, you don't have any leverage to negotiate with your lender for a lower interest rate or principal reduction the way you can with many other forms of consumer debt. Nor is there any related asset you can liquidate to cover the loan. If you find yourself overextended on a car loan, you can always sell the car. If you can't afford your mortgage, you can try to rent out or sell your home.

TIP NO. 2
Know what kind of loans you have.

There are two types of student loans—government and private. Before you can start evaluating the repayment options, you need to determine which kind you have.

Chances are you already know. If you're not sure, check the paperwork: If there's any reference to a Stafford Loan, Perkins Loan, Federal Direct Loan Program, or the Federal Family Education Loan Program, congratulations! You have a government loan, which means you are eligible for a number of different repayment options. This is not the case with private loans. With them, you're basically stuck with the repayment terms that you agreed to when you took the loan out. There's not a lot you can do in the event you have trouble meeting them.

> ### TIP NO. 3
> ### Understand your repayment options.

If you have government loans, you are eligible for two standard repayment plans. The **10-Year Plan** is the default option. You make fixed payments each month for ten years, and at the end of the decade, your loan is paid off and you own your diploma debt free. You can also opt for a **20-Year Plan**, which will stretch out your repayment period. This will lower your monthly payments—but it also will increase the amount of interest you'll pay over the life of the loan. And, of course, it will take you longer to become debt free.

Since your goal in reading this book is to become debt free for life, the 10-year repayment plan is generally your best option. The only reason not to choose it is if you literally can't afford to make the payments (i.e., you have no furniture in your house and are surviving on a diet of government cheese and ramen noodles).

Not surprisingly, as debt loads grow and wages stagnate, the 20-year plan is becoming increasingly popular.

Let's plug in some real numbers to see if this makes sense. Imagine two students who both paid for college with $25,000 federal Stafford loans.

- **Student A** chooses the standard 10-year repayment plan. As a result, he'll have to make monthly payments of $287.70 for ten years, at the end of which he'll be debt free. In all, he will have paid a total of $34,524.14, of which $9,524.14 will have been interest.

- **Student B** chooses the extended 20-year plan. Her monthly payments will be only $190.83. But after 20 years, she will have paid a total of $45,801.70, of which $20,801.70 will have been interest.

In other words, opting for the 20-year repayment plan increases the total amount you will end up paying by roughly a third—in this case, more than $10,000. This is not a good way to get rich!

Your best bet? Enroll in the 10-year repayment plan if you can possibly afford it. The difference between the 10- and 20-year plans on a $25,000 loan will be about $100 per month, an amount you can probably find somewhere (wait tables one night a week, eat out less often, drink fewer lattes, etc.). If you go the 20-year route, my suggestion is that you really work to add extra principal payments to the loan once you have paid down your credit card debt (assuming you have any). Just doubling your minimum payments could get your student loan paid off in less than half the time. Say you've borrowed $20,000 at 6.5% annual interest. Under a 20-year payment program, your minimum monthly payment would be just under $150. If you were to double that and pay $300 each month, instead of taking 20 years to pay off your loan, you'd be done in just seven years—and you'd save nearly $11,000 in interest payments. Keep in mind that as time goes on and you progress in your career, ideally those extra payments will become easier to manage.

THE NON-STANDARD OPTION— INCOME-BASED REPAYMENT

The College Cost Reduction and Access Act of 2007 introduced a third repayment option to the world of federal student loans: income-based repayment, or IBR. The IBR system uses a formula that sets your monthly payment by considering how much you earn and how big a family you have. If this figure turns out to be higher than your required payment under a standard plan, you would obviously want to stick with the standard. But if it's lower, then IBR is a tempting option.

Under IBR, your payment is recalculated each year. If your income goes up, your monthly payment will increase. If it goes down, your monthly payment will fall. At the end of 25 years of making IBR payments, any balance you still owe would be forgiven. (Under current tax law, the amount forgiven would be taxed as income, but who knows what the law will be 25 years from now.)

For example, a single borrower with no family who earns $25,000 per year would have his federal loan payments capped at $109 per month, while a borrower with three dependents (i.e., a family of four) who earns $35,000 per year would have his loan payments capped at just $24 per month.

FinAid, one of the best online resources for information and advice about student loans, has a calculator that will show you how IBR would work out for you. You can check it out at **www.finaid.org/calculators/ibrchart.phtml**.

IBR certainly can sound wonderful—and in some ways it is. It prevents people who are unemployed or earning very low wages from defaulting on their federal student loans. Another advantage is that you can use IBR for a little while and then, if your income goes up, switch back into a standard repayment plan.

This is why many financial experts are pretty high on IBR. But here's the bottom line: If your goal is to get out of debt quickly—i.e., to be debt free for life, not student-loan-free after 25 years—your best bet is *not* IBR. Your best bet is to cut your expenses as much as possible and throw as much money at your loans as possible, while also doing everything you can to keep from accumulating any other kind of debt.

As I see it, IBR should be looked at as a possible tool for borrowers who really can't afford to make their loan payments—not as a way to lower your monthly payments so you can live a more lavish lifestyle.

TIP NO. 4
Consolidate your loans.

Most students who borrow take out multiple loans from multiple sources. After all, there are many different federal direct loan programs, not to mention many private banks that until recently were allowed to make federally insured Perkins and Stafford loans.

Once you graduate, it can become something of a nightmare to keep track of all these loans. This is why most students choose to consolidate their federal loans. (Private student loans are in their own separate universe and cannot be consolidated with federal loans.) Consolidation not only combines all your obligations into one monthly payment, it also cuts down on the paperwork. What's more, there is never a fee for consolidating federal loans and you can choose to extend your repayment term anywhere from 12 to 30 years, depending on how much you borrowed. Of course, stretching out your repayment term is generally not a good option for anyone trying to become debt free for life.

If you have a number of different student loans, you probably also have a number of different interest rates. When you consolidate your loans, your new interest rate is calculated by taking the weighted average of all your old rates (rounded up to the nearest eighth of a percent).

While students with federal loans can consolidate with any lender, it is always a good idea to consolidate into the federal direct loan program. That's because there are some loan forgiveness programs (which we'll deal with in a moment) that are open only to people with federal student loans.

TIP NO. 5

Learn the difference between deferment and forbearance, and check out loan-forgiveness programs.

As I indicated earlier, extending the repayment term on your student loans will cost you thousands of dollars in extra interest charges and delay the day when you finally become debt free. For this reason, I urge you to stick with the 10-year repayment plan unless you truly can't afford it (in which case you might consider switching over to IBR).

That said, it is worth finding out about an increasingly popular option for graduates who have borrowed excessively: deferment and forbearance programs.

The official government website for federal student aid, Student Aid on the Web (**http://studentaid.ed.gov**), defines a deferment as "a temporary suspension of loan payments for specific situations such as reenrollment in school, unemployment, or economic hardship."

If you have subsidized federal loans, this can be a very good deal, since interest will not accrue during a deferment. However, if your loans are unsubsidized, interest will accrue.

If you don't qualify for deferment but are experiencing financial difficulty, you can apply for forbearance, which will temporarily postpone or reduce your payments. The catch here is that interest will continue to accrue even if your loans are subsidized. Note that loan servicers do not have to grant forbearances or deferments in all situations, and that you still have to make payments while you wait for them to make the decision.

Most private student lenders also offer forbearance and deferment options, but there are no uniform policies governing private student loans and you are completely at the lender's mercy. Check with your lender to find out your options.

Here's the problem with forbearance: While you aren't making payments, you'll continue to be charged interest. This unpaid interest gets added to the total amount you owe; the more you owe, the more interest you get charged, and the more your debt grows. This is called negative amortization: You end up owing more money every month, and the amount of that increase goes up every month as well. Trust me when I tell you this can rise up and bite you in the financial butt, so make sure you know exactly what you are getting into if you go this route!

Loan Forgiveness

Loan forgiveness programs do just what the name indicates— if you qualify for one, your student loan can be completely forgiven, meaning whatever balance remains will be wiped out without penalty. One of the best-known loan-forgiveness programs is for federal employees. If you work for the federal government for ten years and make 120 on-time monthly payments, any remaining balances you owe on federal student loans will be forgiven. (This also applies to people who work for municipal governments or hold certain positions in the non-profit world; check with the Department of Education for details.) Of course, if you're signed up for a 10-year repayment plan, this will happen regardless of what kind of work you do.

Many states offer their own programs that help public employees pay off their student loans, but a word of warning:
These programs can quickly evaporate in times of financial
crisis. And with so many states facing unprecedented deficits and a gloomy long-term economic outlook, this is exactly
what is happening.

In May 2009, the *New York Times* reported the sad case of
a young Kentucky couple, both schoolteachers, who had borrowed a total of $100,000 to pay for college and enrolled in
a program to have their loans forgiven. Unfortunately, their
program was cut and their forgiveness wound up being a fraction of what they had thought it would be.

You can find more information about loan-forgiveness
programs on the FinAid website at **www.finaid.org/loans/
forgiveness.phtml**.

TIP NO. 6
Ditch your loans asap
(especially your private ones).

The bottom line with student loans is this: The fastest way to
get rid of them is to live beneath your means and pay them
off as quickly as you can. This is particularly true if you have
taken out private student loans. If you've got private loans and
you want to have any chance of finishing rich, it is imperative
that you move paying them off to the top of your list of financial priorities.

The main reason why you should want private loans out
of your life as quickly as possible is that their adjustable rates
make them ticking time bombs. You usually sign up for a student loan when you first enter college, and with a variable rate,
you have no way of predicting what your payments will be

when you graduate in four (or five or six) years. This is a terribly speculative way to finance your education and it's one of the reasons that an increasing number of financial experts are advising students not to use private student loans at all. Another reason is that the lack of consumer protections means private borrowers are generally at the mercy of their lenders.

So if you have both private and federal loans, I believe you should make paying off the private loans your first priority—even if the interest rates on the private loans might currently be lower. Planning to pay them off over 10 or 20 years is just way too risky—and because of the lingering effects of the credit crunch, refinancing them into fixed-rate debt is nearly impossible.

In fact, if you have a mix of private and federal loans, I would recommend that you use IBR or an extended payment plan to keep your federal loan payments as low as possible and throw all the money you can at your private loans. They're that dangerous.

Speaking of danger, I would also warn parents not to go out on too much of a financial limb to finance their children's college education. The single biggest mistake most parents make when it comes to Junior's college funding is making it too much of a priority. Sending your kids to college is important, but you should think long and hard before you take out a second mortgage to cover their tuition—and you should *not* put it ahead of your own retirement needs. Remember, the greatest gift you can give your children is to ensure that you won't be a financial burden to them.

> **TIP NO. 7**
> ### Don't forget to deduct your interest costs when you file your taxes.

I hear from people all the time who have been diligently paying off their student loans for years—only to discover that they had either forgotten or not realized in the first place that they're eligible for the income-tax deduction on student loan interest. This deduction is calculated as an adjustment to income, so unlike the home mortgage interest deduction, you do not need to itemize your deductions in order to qualify for it.

You can claim up to $2,500 in interest (not principal) as a tax deduction provided that you meet the following requirements:

- You paid interest on a qualified student loan in the last tax year. (If you did, you should receive a form 1098-E from your lender.)

- Your filing status is not married filing separately.

- Your modified adjusted gross income is less than $70,000 ($145,000 if filing jointly).

- You and your spouse, if filing jointly, cannot be claimed as dependents on someone else's return.

Assuming you're in a 25% tax bracket, this deduction could save you as much as $625 per year.

> **TIP NO. 8**
> ## Think before you borrow.

If you haven't yet taken the plunge to borrow money for school but are considering it, then consider this: You need to think through what is a reasonable amount to borrow for an education.

Financial aid expert Mark Kantrowitz, the founder of FinAid.org, advises students to limit their borrowing to an amount equal to the annual salary they expect to make their first year out of school. The problem with this approach is that it requires you to predict your income four, five, or six years down the road—and be right not only about the economic outlook, but also about the kind of job (if any) you're going to wind up having.

A better approach would be to keep your borrowing to the absolute minimum and never, ever take out any private student loans. The fact is that dependent undergraduate students can borrow as much as $27,000 through the federal Stafford loan program over four years, while independent students (usually students who are over age 25 or married) can borrow $45,000. If that isn't enough for you to be able to afford college, you should probably rethink your choice of school. Don't sentence yourself to a lifetime of indentured servitude in pursuit of a sweatshirt with a nice name on it. This may sound harsh, but student loans should cover only a small portion of your college costs. There are plenty of other, better ways to pay for college—among them, savings plans, scholarships, and part-time employment. Remember, people have been working their way through college for as long as they've been giving out degrees.

If there is an exception to this rule, it involves the most prestigious medical, law, and business schools. Graduates of these elite schools tend to be able to manage their debt loads: Very few Wharton MBAs wind up defaulting on their student loans. That said, I'm a realist. I know most people will borrow whatever it takes to go to the school they want to go to—but please, really consider the pressure you're putting yourself under when you graduate with a huge load of debt on your shoulders. Dealing with it is much harder than most young people think and most parents realize.

TIP NO. 9
Do your homework and shop around for the best loan.

I put this tip last because, as I just noted, if you are reading this book, it's more than likely that you've already gotten your student loans. However, if you haven't, then make sure you do your homework—and shop around. There are a mind-numbing variety of programs, each with a mind-numbing set of rules and conditions. The difference between the wrong loan and the right one can be the difference between a miserable life and a great one.

Here are some tips on where to go for information and help.

Federal Loans

Federal student loans are a standardized product, and the best route to one is through the school you are looking to attend. Reach out to the student-aid department for information about the various programs and how to apply.

Private Loans

If for some reason you have to go the route of getting a student loan from a private lender, there isn't a better resource for information and advice than FinAid (**www.finaid.org**). This website contains everything you need to know about borrowing money for private student loans.

Scholarships

FastWeb (**www.FastWeb.com**) bills itself as "the leading scholarship search provider for every student, whether you're in high school or a mother of two returning to school," and with 34 million users, the boast is probably justified. This amazing website contains everything you need to find help quickly about both scholarships and college loans.

A COLLEGE DEGREE CAN CHANGE YOUR LIFE— BUT SO CAN DEBT

Getting a college degree is one of the most powerful things a person can do to improve his or her life: It broadens your horizons, gives you career flexibility, sets you up to earn more money, and provides numerous other psychic benefits. But if you finance college by borrowing too much—or if you mismanage the debt you have incurred—the benefits of a higher education can be quickly outstripped by its costs.

I'm personally in favor of getting the best education you can afford—but the key word is "afford"! Too often we borrow more than is really necessary for college. If you have to borrow money to attend the school of your choice, consider whether or not the additional cost is worth the extra burden of debt you will take on. Remember, it's a debt you will probably be paying off for at least a decade or two.

DEBT FREE FOR LIFE ACTION STEPS

❏ Make sure you know what kind of student loans you have and what the payment options are.
❏ If you have a number of different government-backed student loans, consolidate them.
❏ If you are having trouble paying off your student loans, check out which loan-forgiveness programs may be available to you.
❏ Make it a priority to pay off any private student loans you may have.

CHAPTER ELEVEN

ERASE YOUR DEBT
WITH THREE SIMPLE WORDS:
"TIME-BARRED DEBT"

What would you say if I told you there was a totally legal way to get rid of some or all of your debt IMMEDIATELY—without having to declare bankruptcy, ruin your credit score, or pay big fees to a lawyer?

I know. By now, you've learned that if something sounds too good to be true, it probably is. But there are a few exceptions to that commonsense rule—and this is one of them.

Now before I share this incredible information, please know that I am not a lawyer—and I am not giving legal advice here. Neither am I suggesting that anyone borrow money and not pay it back. But I am your advocate—and you deserve to know the truth about your legal rights so you can make the appropriate decisions for yourself. Just remember this: Before you do anything based on the information in this chapter, please consult an attorney! This chapter is filled with web addresses to visit and telephone numbers to call to get help.

SIMPLE FAIRNESS SAYS YOU SHOULD
BE ABLE TO GET ON WITH YOUR LIFE

You're probably familiar with the idea of a statute of limitations. A statute of limitations is a law that sets a limit on how much time you have after an offense has been committed to take legal action against someone. For example, in many states, the statute of limitations on grand theft is six years—meaning that the authorities have six years after, say, a car has been stolen to charge somebody with that particular crime. Once six years have passed, the thief can breathe easy; if he hasn't already been caught, he's home free. The authorities can no longer prosecute him.

The same goes for civil actions. In California, for example, the statute of limitations on personal injury is two years. So if you're at the gym and someone drops a barbell on your foot, you have two years to take them to court. If you miss the deadline, you're out of luck. No matter how open-and-shut your case may be, once those two years are up, you no longer have the right to sue the guy who broke your big toe.

This may seem kind of arbitrary, but there are actually good reasons for it. For one thing, the longer a case drags on, the more likely it is that evidence will be lost or damaged, that memories will fade, and that the truth will be harder to determine. But perhaps even more important, our basic sense of fairness includes the notion that after a reasonable amount of time, potential defendants should either be charged or allowed to get on with their lives. People shouldn't have to live indefinitely with the possibility that they might one day be hauled into court.

JUST BECAUSE YOU STILL OWE IT, DOESN'T MEAN THEY CAN COLLECT IT

So what does all this have to do with getting out of debt? Well, believe it or not, there is a statute of limitations on debts. It's not that you no longer owe the money after a certain amount of time. The only way to really get rid of a legitimate debt is to pay it off or declare bankruptcy. But under state and federal law, most creditors have only a limited amount of time—typically between three and ten years, depending on where you live and what kind of debt it is—in which they can sue you to collect. What this means is that once any particular debt of yours ages past the deadline, it becomes effectively uncollectible—and you are effectively off the hook.

The legal term for this is "time-barred debt." A time-barred debt is any debt that has been past due for longer than the applicable statute of limitations. You still owe the money, but there is nothing your creditor can legally do to force you to pay it. So with this in mind, what you want to do is look at all your debts and see if any of them are time-barred. If they are, you can relax. Given that debts more than five years old carry less weight with the credit bureaus—and fall off your credit report completely after seven years to ten years—they probably already impacted your credit score and eventually they will drop off (if they haven't already).

WHAT TYPE OF DEBT DO YOU HAVE?

The rules governing time-barred debt are complicated and they vary from state to state. But if you put your mind to it, they are not all that hard to follow. Here's what you have to do.

First off, you need to figure out what kind of debt you have. Basically, debt comes in several different flavors. There are loans based on oral contracts (usually an informal "handshake agreement" with a friend or relative), loans based on written contracts (formal agreements that include the general terms), loans based on promissory notes (like a mortgage or auto loan, where the payment schedule and interest charges are spelled out), and what are called open-ended loans (revolving lines of credit that don't have to be paid off by any specific date; this includes *all* credit card accounts).

Each of these types of debt has its own statute of limitations. In most states, the statute of limitations on oral debts and open-ended loans varies between three and six years. For written contracts and promissory notes, the typical length is between four and ten years. But there are plenty of exceptions. In Kentucky and Ohio, for example, the statute of limitations on written contracts and promissory notes is 15 years. So you need to determine the rules for your particular state.

The way to find out for sure is to check with the office of your state's Attorney General. (Contact information for state Attorneys General is available on the website of the National Association of Attorneys General at **www.naag.org**.) There are also many unofficial websites that provide tables listing every state's statute of limitations for all four types of debt. Here are three good ones:

- **About.com** *http://credit.about.com/od/statuteoflimitations/a/entirestatesol.htm*

- **Bankrate.com** *www.bankrate.com/finance/credit-cards/state-statutes-of-limitations-for-old-debts-2.aspx*

- **CreditInfoCenter.com** *www.creditinfocenter.com/rebuild/statuteLimitations.shtml*

Keep in mind that not all debt has a statute of limitations! There is NO statute of limitations on federal student loans, most fines, some tax bills, and all child-support obligations.

Here's a state-by-state breakdown of how long the statute of limitations is for different kinds of debts.

State	Oral Contracts	Written Contracts	Promissory Notes	Open-Ended Accounts
AK	6	6	3	3
AL	6	6	6	3
AR	5	5	5	3
AZ	3	6	6	3
CA	2	4	4	4
CO	6	6	6	3
CT	3	6	6	6
DC	3	3	3	3
DE	3	3	3	4
FL	4	5	5	4
GA	4	6	6	4
HI	6	6	6	6
IA	5	10	5	5
ID	4	5	5	4
IL	5	10	10	5
IN	6	10	10	6
KS	3	5	5	3
KY	5	15	15	5
LA	10	10	10	3
MA	6	6	6	6
MD	3	3	6	3
ME	6	6	6	6
MI	6	6	6	6
MN	6	6	6	6

MO	5	10	10	5
MS	3	3	3	3
MT	3	8	8	5
NC	3	3	5	4
ND	6	6	6	6
NE	4	5	5	4
NH	3	3	6	3
NJ	6	6	6	6
NM	4	6	6	4
NV	4	6	3	4
NY	6	6	6	6
OH	6	15	15	6
OK	3	5	5	3
OR	6	6	6	6
PA	4	6	4	6
RI	10	10	6	4
SC	3	3	3	3
SD	6	6	6	6
TN	6	4	6	6
TX	4	4	4	4
UT	4	6	6	4
VA	3	6	6	3
VT	6	6	5	4
WA	3	6	6	3
WI	6	6	10	6
WV	5	15	6	4
WY	8	10	10	8

Source: PoorCreditGenie.com/crsstatutelim.html

MAKE SURE YOU KNOW
WHEN THE CLOCK STARTED TICKING

Once you know what type of debt you have and what statute of limitations applies, you need to figure out when the deadline clock started ticking. Generally speaking, the countdown begins when you violate your loan agreement—usually the first time you miss a payment deadline. But that's not a hard-and-fast rule. If you make any kind of payment later on or charge something to the account or do anything that shows you recognize that you owe the debt, the clock will stop and reset to zero.

Under these circumstances, the countdown would start over again on the account's "date of last activity." For a credit card debt, this would most likely be the last time you used the card or made a payment.

JUST BECAUSE THEY CAN'T SUE YOU
DOESN'T MEAN THEY WON'T TRY

Even though a creditor can't take you to court to collect a time-barred debt, that doesn't mean he's going to give up. There are a number of wrinkles in the law, and determined debt collectors are always trying to exploit them. For instance, debtors are covered only by the statute of limitations of the state in which they currently live, not where they originally borrowed the money. So if you move from a state with a short statute of limitations to a state with a long one, you could find that what you thought was a time-barred debt isn't one any longer.

And even if you don't move and your debt is clearly time-barred, that doesn't mean your creditor can't still continue to call you up and send you letters demanding payment. Even worse, the outfit you originally borrowed the money from may write the loan off and sell it to a full-time debt collector. In fact, this is almost always what happens with debts you have owed for a long time. Debt collection is a multibillion-dollar industry. There are investors known as "vultures" who buy debt from banks and other creditors all day long, hoping that if they can buy your debt for 10 cents on the dollar, they can collect 20 cents—which would give them a 100% profit before expenses.

Their expenses, by the way, are low. All they do is fill rooms with professional (and sometimes not so professional) cold-callers who are paid usually minimum wage plus a commission on the debt they manage to collect. These guys tend to be pit bulls. Time-barred or not, they will pull out all the stops trying to get you to pay.

The good news is that federal law protects you from being harassed by debt collectors. Under the Fair Debt Collection Practices Act, debt collectors are not allowed to engage in any unfair, deceptive, or abusive practices while collecting debts. Among other things, debt collectors aren't allowed to contact you at inconvenient times, such as before 8 in the morning or after 9 at night, unless you agree to it. They're also not allowed to telephone you at work if you tell them (verbally or in writing) that you're not allowed to get calls there.

Here's a partial list of what else the law says bill collectors can't do. (You can find a full list online at **www.ftc.gov/bcp/edu/pubs/consumer/credit/cre18.shtm**.)

- Debt collectors aren't allowed to harass or abuse you. This includes:
  - ▸ Using threats of violence or harm

- ▸ Using obscene or profane language
- ▸ Driving you crazy with repeated phone calls

- Debt collectors aren't allowed to lie to you. This includes:
  - ▸ Falsely claiming that they are attorneys or government representatives
  - ▸ Falsely claiming that you have broken the law
  - ▸ Falsely claiming they work for a credit-reporting company
  - ▸ Misrepresenting how much you owe
  - ▸ Falsely claiming you will be arrested if you don't pay your debt
  - ▸ Falsely claiming that they'll seize your property or garnish your wages unless they are permitted by law to do this and actually intend to do so

- Debt collectors aren't allowed to give false credit information about you to anyone, including a credit-reporting company.

- Debt collectors aren't allowed to use a false company name or send you anything that looks like an official document from a court or government agency if that's not what it really is.

- Debt collectors aren't allowed to engage in unfair practices. These include:
  - ▸ Making you pay any additional money (whether in the form of interest, fees, or special charges) that's not specified in your original loan agreement or allowed by state law
  - ▸ Depositing a postdated check early
  - ▸ Contacting you by postcard

And while the law does not prohibit anyone from trying to collect time-barred debts, as long as they do not sue or threaten to sue you, it does give you the ability to make them leave you alone.

HOW TO GET A DEBT COLLECTOR OFF YOUR BACK

Amazingly enough, there is a really simple way to stop debt collectors from bugging you to repay a time-barred debt, even though you do legally owe the money. All you have to do is send them a letter telling them to stop contacting you. Once you tell them that (in writing, of course), they've got to get off your back. The only contact they're allowed to have with you from then on is either to confirm that they are going to leave you alone or to let you know that they are going to take some specific action against you. Of course, since they can't sue you over a time-barred debt, there really isn't any action they can take.

HERE'S WHAT THE FTC SAYS!

This is what the FTC says on its website about what you should put in a letter to a creditor regarding time-barred debt.

> According to the law, if you send the debt collector a letter stating that you do not owe some or all of the money within 30 days after you receive written notice of a debt, the collector must stop trying to collect until you've been given written verification of the debt, like a copy of the bill for the amount you supposedly owe. The collector can renew collection activities once you've gotten proof of the debt.

You can stop debt collectors from contacting you about any debt, regardless of whether you owe it, by writing a letter telling them to stop contacting you. Once the collector gets your letter, it may not contact you again—except to say there will be no further contact or to let you know that the collector or creditor intends to take some specific action. Sending a letter doesn't absolve you of the debt if you actually owe it; the debt collector or creditor still could sue you for the debt.

Make a copy of the letter for yourself and send the original via certified mail with return receipt requested. You want to be able to prove the letter was sent and received in case the debt collector ignores your instructions and you wind up having to file a complaint or lawsuit against him.

DON'T MAKE THIS MISTAKE— IT CAN RESTART THE CLOCK!

One thing you should never do when you're dealing with a creditor regarding a time-barred debt is agree to a payment plan or actually make a payment. Doing this—or anything else that in effect acknowledges that you owe them money— can reset or restart the statute of limitations clock!

This is often the ultimate scam that debt collectors use. They call you up, get you to admit that this debt is yours, and then ask you to sign up for a debt-repayment plan that might require you to pay as little as 20 cents on the dollar of what you owe. It may sound good in theory, but it can backfire big time. This is because if your debt has already passed the "point of no return," there is no legal action the debt collector can take to make you pay any of it. However, if you agree to a payment plan, the statute of limitations clock starts ticking all over again—which means they can go to court and get a judgment against you.

I recently worked with a woman named Jennifer who owed $30,000 in past-due credit card debt. A debt collector offered to reduce her obligation to just $5,000 if she wired him a check in that amount immediately.

Sound like a good deal? Guess again. Jennifer lived in Texas and her debt was five years old. Guess what? In Texas, the statute of limitations on "open accounts" (i.e., credit cards) is four years. In other words, there was nothing the debt collector could do legally to force her to pay any of that debt anymore. Most important, the debt collector who was harassing her knew this! The debt had already been charged off by the credit card company and the debt collector was nothing more than a vulture who bought her debt for pennies on the dollar.

So what Jennifer did was write the debt collector a letter pointing out that the alleged debt was more than four years old and hence time-barred in the state of Texas, and so could they please stop bothering her about it.

As a result of this one letter, the collector never called her again.

DEBT COLLECTORS ARE NOT YOUR FRIENDS— DON'T GET SUCKED IN

While some debt collectors come down on you like a ton of bricks, others are more subtle. Instead of trying to intimidate you into paying a time-barred debt, they will attempt to sweet-talk you into cooperating. One common tactic is to offer to give you extra time to pay off the debt or to suggest that you make a small "token payment" just to prove you're a good guy. Don't be taken in.

As I noted earlier, **doing anything to acknowledge that you owe the money—especially agreeing to a payment plan or actually making a payment—can reset or restart the statute of limitations clock.** And that would allow a creditor to get a judgment against you, which could leave you with your bank accounts seized or your wages garnished.

So if you have any time-barred debt, the only response you should have to a creditor's demand for payment is a polite "thanks for calling, but I can't help you" along the lines I suggested earlier.

Another possible response is to say to them, "PROVE IT TO ME. Send me written documentation that proves I owe this money."

The great truth is that many of the collection agencies that call you don't have any proof (and they know it). All they generally have is a long list of names and numbers that they've purchased from a bank or other lender that has given up trying to get paid back. They don't actually have any proof of the debt, such as copies of the loan agreement you may have signed.

Many attorneys who help people with time-barred debt generally advise clients who have debts that are not yet time-barred but are close to reaching the statute of limitations to lay low and don't do or say anything in response to a creditor that could be construed as admitting you owe the money. Remember, time is on your side, and the vultures who bought your debt from the credit card companies that wrote off your debt know this, which is why they will illegally harass you. Don't let them!

DEBT IS A RIGHTS ISSUE—
AND YOU HAVE RIGHTS!

Let me say that I believe in living a life of integrity. When you borrow money, you should pay it back. You made a promise to do just that, and you should always keep your promises. That said, I'm also your advocate. If you owe a debt that your state's statute of limitations defines as "time-barred," you deserve to know what your rights are. What's more, you are entitled to use those rights to get out of debt and get back on your feet financially.

I'm also enough of a realist to know that much of the money that debt collectors try to collect these days isn't what was originally borrowed. It's the result of outrageous interest and nonsense fees that were tacked on later. I worked with one couple who had borrowed about $10,000 on their credit card—and had made $14,000 in payments. Nonetheless, what with interest and penalties, they still owed more than $25,000. Now that's just wrong. So I say—use your rights!

LAST BUT NOT LEAST

If your debt isn't time-barred and you can't use this little-known legal right, don't fear—this book contains plenty of other strategies you can use to crush your debt and live a Debt Free Life. So keep reading—and don't forget this strategy just because it may not apply to you. Share it with friends if they are being hounded by creditors. You could wind up saving them a fortune.

YOU DON'T HAVE TO DO IT YOURSELF

As I said before, I believe that just about everything I have suggested in this book, from understanding your rights with time-barred debt to DOLPing your way to financial freedom, is stuff you can do yourself. That said, I have plenty of readers and friends who would rather not do this on their own—who feel more comfortable working with a professional.

A very close friend of mine, who owed more than $100,000 in credit card debt and was just weeks away from bankruptcy, knew he couldn't do it himself. But instead of getting depressed, he went to a non-profit credit-counseling group. They saved his life financially. Today, he is completely debt free!

My friend's story is not unusual. Millions of people have gone this route with similar results. So with this in mind, let's look at how these groups work and how to choose one if doing it yourself isn't right for you.

DEBT FREE FOR LIFE ACTION STEPS

❑ Check out the statute of limitations on unpaid debts in your state.

❑ Check to see if you have any debts that have been past due for longer than the applicable statute of limitations.

❑ If you do, figure out when the "deadline clock" started ticking.

❑ Instruct any debt collectors trying to get you to pay a time-barred debt to stop bothering you.

❑ Before you do anything, consult with an attorney.

CHAPTER TWELVE

HOW TO GET NON-PROFIT CREDIT COUNSELING—AND A PROFESSIONAL TO GUIDE YOU OUT OF DEBT

Not everyone has the knowledge and the discipline to get out of debt by themselves. Many people—maybe you're one of them—need someone to take them by the hand and walk them out of debt. There is nothing wrong with this.

So if after reading this book and trying my DOLP Method or the DebtWise.com service I described in Chapters Five and Six, you don't feel you can do this by yourself, or you simply don't want to do it yourself, by all means get someone to help you. Just keep in mind that you need to find the right person. That's where this chapter comes in.

My recommendation, if you decide you need some outside help, is that you consider working with a non-profit credit-counseling agency. It may take a little extra effort to find a good one, but it's not that hard and the benefits can be enormous. As I'll share in a moment, my best friend Bob did just that—and in less than five years with the help of a non-profit credit counselor, he freed himself from more than $100,000 in credit card debt! And he's not alone.

MILLIONS OF PEOPLE TURN TO NON-PROFIT CREDIT-COUNSELING AGENCIES EVERY YEAR

According to the two major non-profit credit-counseling trade associations—the National Foundation for Credit Counseling

(NFCC) and the Association of Independent Consumer Credit Counseling Agencies (AICCCA)—some eight million people came to member agencies for help in 2009. So if you are reading this book and need help—trust me, there's no reason to be embarrassed. You've got plenty of company.

In this chapter I will explain how non-profit credit counseling works and how it can help you. Among other things, I will cover the following:

- What is non-profit credit counseling?

- What exactly does a non-profit credit counselor do for you?

- How do you go about finding a non-profit credit counselor you can trust?

- What are the costs associated with non-profit credit counseling?

I hope you noticed that whenever I refer to credit counseling, I also use the word "non-profit." That's because I want to emphasize that what I'm talking about here *isn't* the for-profit "Debt Settlement" industry. We'll deal with the for-profit companies later in Chapter Thirteen. This chapter is solely about non-profit credit counselors—and non-profit credit counseling is completely different from the for-profit version. *I do not recommend that you use (or even consider) for-profit credit counseling UNTIL you have already tried non-profit credit counseling.*

GOING FROM A SIX-FIGURE CREDIT CARD DEBT
TO BEING DEBT FREE

I mentioned earlier that a good friend of mine got out from under more than $100,000 in credit card debt by working with a non-profit credit-counseling agency. My friend's name is Bob, and just a few days before I wrote this chapter, he and I celebrated his "Debt Freedom Day"—his making the final payment that took care of the last of his credit card debt. Here's what he said to me after he put the check in the mail: "David, I now feel like Superman. It's amazing what being out of debt can do for your spirit and your energy."

Considering that five years earlier Bob was considering bankruptcy and feeling totally defeated, his success story is truly AMAZING.

Indeed, Bob's experience was so amazing that it made me see the credit-counseling industry in a totally new light. Before I saw Bob turn his life around with the help of a non-profit credit counselor, I was skeptical of the industry. I had heard too many horror stories about people who had been victimized by debt counselors and it was hard to really know whom you could trust. But Bob's experience—and that of many others like him—changed my mind.

As I said, Bob and I are best friends. We met in grade school and went all the way through high school together. We have the kind of friendship where you feel like you're family. So I usually knew everything that was going on with Bob, including the fact that he was having great success at work and earning a six-figure salary.

So imagine my shock on a crisp New York morning at breakfast with Bob, when he broke down and told me he was in big trouble. In truth, I never would have guessed the problem would be debt. As I said, I was under the impression that Bob was doing really well at work. But that morning Bob told me what was really happening: His business had slowed down, his spending hadn't—and he now owed SIX FIGURES in credit card debt. He had already refinanced his home multiple times and borrowed from his 401(k) plan.

To say he was in deep financial trouble was an understatement. He was literally down to his last few thousand dollars.

HIS INCOME HAD DROPPED, BUT HIS SPENDING HADN'T

Considering that I hear stories like this every day from readers—not to mention people on the street who recognize me from television—Bob's news shouldn't have come as a shock. But I hadn't seen the signs. Bob and I spent a lot of time together. We ate out together, traveled together, shopped together. And then it hit me. Of course I hadn't seen the signs. Bob's behavior hadn't changed. What had changed was something I had no knowledge about—his income. His income had dropped, but his spending hadn't.

As Bob explained the details, I knew there wouldn't be any quick fix here. I told him over coffee that I thought he could get out of this mess without having to declare bankruptcy, but he would need to get brutally serious abut his situation—and he would need to act quickly. "I can give you my tools," I said to him, "but I think you're going to need more help than that. I think you will need to find a non-profit credit counselor." The challenge, I added, would be finding the right counselor.

As we parted company that morning, I asked Bob how long it had taken him to rack up his debt. Bob said it had been about three years.

"Then you should assume it will take you at least three years—and maybe more—to get out," I said. "But if you are committed, you *will* get out—and the time will go by faster than you can imagine."

Bob *was* committed, and things turned out just as I had hoped they would. He found a terrific non-profit credit-counseling agency, which renegotiated the terms of his debts with his creditors and got him into a debt-management plan. Every month without fail, he sent the agency a chunk of money, which it used to make all his payments. At the same time, he stopped using his credit cards and learned to live on cash and a debit card.

As I type these words, it's amazing to me that five years have passed so quickly since Bob and I had that talk over breakfast. Today, Bob is out of debt. That's quite the financial turnaround. And I can't take any credit for it. The credit goes completely to Bob (because he committed to changing his life and his spending) and to the non-profit counseling agency (which helped him do what needed to be done).

So now let's see if this could be the right path for you.

WHAT EXACTLY IS
NON-PROFIT CREDIT COUNSELING?

What non-profit credit-counseling agencies do is work with you and your creditors to make it possible for you to pay off all your debts—usually within three to five years. They don't reduce the amount you owe, but as was the case with Bob, they can help you develop better financial habits—and, if necessary, they can get your creditors to cut your interest rates and often waive penalty fees, which can bring your monthly payments way down.

What distinguishes non-profit credit-counseling agencies from other kinds of debt-relief companies is that they are certified by the IRS as being non-profit organizations. This doesn't mean their services are free—or that earning money isn't important to them. They simply have a different type of financial structure, and the benefit to you, the consumer, is that it generally costs a lot less to work with them than with a for-profit debt counselor.

There are hundreds of these non-profit organizations throughout the United States. Some are small mom-and-pop businesses, while others are extremely large operations with hundreds of employees and thousands of clients. As I'll discuss later, the best ones tend to belong to one of the two major non-profit credit-counseling trade associations, the National Foundation for Credit Counseling (NFCC) or the Association of Independent Consumer Credit Counseling Agencies (AICCCA).

HOW DO YOU KNOW IF YOU NEED A CREDIT COUNSELOR?

You may be a good candidate for credit counseling if any or all of the following apply to you.

- After reading this book and putting in place either the DOLP Plan or the DebtWise.com plan, you still feel you could use some hand-holding.

- You are having trouble making your monthly minimum payments and you can't consistently pay your bills on time.

- Interest payments are eating you alive, and you've been unable to get the credit card companies to work with you on lowering them.

If any of this sounds familiar, credit counseling may be what you need. With this in mind, let's take a look at exactly what a good non-profit credit counselor can do for you.

EIGHT WAYS A GREAT NON-PROFIT CREDIT-COUNSELING AGENCY CAN HELP YOU

1. They will offer you a free counseling session.

Before they ask you to sign up for anything, most good non-profit credit-counseling agencies will spend at least 60 to 90 minutes with you reviewing your entire debt situation and overall financial position FOR FREE. (Some reputable firms do charge an up-front consultation fee, but it's very small— usually less than $100.) This initial discussion can take place over the phone or in person. But whichever it is, before the counselor gets into the nuts and bolts of your situation, he or she will probably start with a "holistic approach" to understand your situation better. A common first question is, "What brings you to us today?" This not only helps to break the ice, but, equally important, it also allows the counselor to really hear your story. They may then ask you about your goals—what do you really want to accomplish with a debt counselor? What are your short-term and long-term financial objectives? The idea is to encourage you to think beyond the immediate problem of getting out of debt and start looking forward to a brighter future.

2. They will help you look closely at your financial reality.

Once they have an idea of what brought you to them, a good agency will start evaluating your finances. First, they will look at what you earn and what your expenses are. Then they will look closely at your debt, how much you owe, what kind of interest rates you are paying, and how much you are wasting in late fees and over-the-limit penalties. Based on all this, they can figure out if you might be able to get yourself out of debt simply by changing your financial habits, or if you need to enroll in what's known as a Debt Management Plan (or DMP), where they negotiate directly with your creditors to work out an arrangement designed to make it possible for you to get out of debt within three to five years.

3. They will create a spending plan or budget for you.

Ultimately, there's no point in trying to pay down your debt if you don't at the same time create a spending plan that allows you to live within your means. Creating this plan or budget is a critical part of what a really good non-profit counselor will do for you. They will study where your money is going and make recommendations about where you can and should cut back in order to live within your means.

4. They will work with you on "secured debt" as well as credit card debt.

As we discussed earlier, there are two basic forms of debt: secured debt, where you put up collateral (such as a home mortgage or car loan), and unsecured debt, where you don't (most commonly credit card debt). A good counselor will review both your secured debt and your unsecured debt. The goal will be first to stabilize your financial life at home—that is, make sure you can buy groceries, keep the lights on, and pay your rent or mortgage. Then they will look at what's the best way to deal with your credit card debt and other unsecured obligations.

> ### 5. They will be prepared to recommend a DMP—
> ### but only if it makes sense for you.

Earlier, I mentioned the term "Debt Management Plan," or DMP. A DMP is a payment plan that your credit counselor negotiates with your creditors to help you get out of debt. Literally millions of cash-strapped credit card customers have been enrolled in such plans in the last few years.

In most cases, a DMP will do the following:

- It will create a three- to five-year plan to get your debt paid off.

- It will lower the interest rate on your debt—usually to below 10% and sometimes much lower. I have coached people who had their interest rates cut from 29% to *zero* as a result of enrolling in a DMP.

- It will get your credit card company to stop charging you the over-the-limit fees, annual membership fees, and late-payment penalties.

- It will freeze your credit card accounts (meaning you can't use your cards anymore) until your balances have been paid off. Some credit card companies will actually close your account and make you apply for a new card once your debt is paid off.

A reputable non-profit organization won't recommend a DMP to just anyone. According to the National Foundation for Credit Counseling, about one out of every four people who come to one of their member agencies is able to "sustain a DMP." The fact is that a DMP can't really help you if your debt is so large—or your income is so low—that even after your interest rates are lowered and your penalty fees are waived, you still can't afford to make your payments. That's why it's critical to have a counselor who will really look closely at your overall financial situation before making any recommendations.

6. They will level with you if they think you may need to file for bankruptcy.

According to the NFCC, about 10% of all credit-counseling clients probably should consider bankruptcy. (We'll cover the ins and outs of bankruptcy and how to find a good bankruptcy attorney in Chapter Fourteen.) A good credit-counseling agency will let you know right away if this is your situation. Under the Bankruptcy Abuse Prevention and Consumer Protection Act of 2005, you're not allowed to file for bankruptcy without first working with an approved credit-counseling agency, and a good agency will provide you with legally required pre-filing counseling. What a good counseling agency won't do is recommend a specific bankruptcy lawyer. They may provide a list of qualified attorneys or legal resources, but they will not push you to use any particular one.

7. They will be able to provide you with references and testimonials.

Most reputable non-profit credit counselors take great pride in the success stories of their customers—and they should be ready and willing to provide you with references from people like you whom they have helped. If you're considering a credit-counseling agency that wasn't recommended to you by someone you know, ask them for the names of three former clients whose situations were similar to yours who might be willing to talk to you about their experiences.

8. They will happily explain their fees up front.

Any honest, accredited non-profit credit-counseling agency will be happy to explain exactly how much they charge—and to put it in writing. As I noted earlier, many won't charge you anything for the first appointment, and those that do generally ask for less than $100. In most cases, you will have to pay a monthly fee if you enter a DMP, but this, too, should be nominal—usually $50 a month or less. If you can't afford to pay, most non-profit consumer counseling organizations will still work with you. Both the NFCC and AICCCA membership guidelines say that consumers cannot be denied service based on inability to pay. According to the NFCC, most of its member agencies do not charge a fee for counseling, and even among those that do, if a client requests that the fee be waived, it generally will be.

WHAT A GOOD NON-PROFIT
CREDIT-COUNSELING AGENCY WON'T DO

- They won't pressure you to sign up with them.

- They won't charge you a huge sign-up fee. (It shouldn't be more than $100.)

- They won't charge you a huge fee each month. (In most cases, it should be $50 or less.)

- They won't tell you to stop making your monthly credit card or other debt payments so they can negotiate a better deal for you.

- They won't tell you they can sue the credit card company on your behalf.

- They won't recommend that you enroll in a DMP before they have taken a good look at your overall financial picture.

HOW NON-PROFIT COUNSELING AGENCIES
MAKE MONEY

If you're at all like me, you may be wondering how exactly non-profit credit-counseling agencies are able to provide all the services they do at such a low cost to the consumer—and often at no cost at all?

The answer isn't simple—but it is important to know. First and foremost, many non-profit credit-counseling agencies re-

ceive grants from a variety of federal, state, and local government agencies as well as from private foundations. In addition,
creditors (that is, the folks to whom you owe the money) make
what are called "fair share contributions" to the agencies. To
put it another way, they pay the credit-counseling agency a
percentage of the debt that the agency helps them to settle.
These contributions amount to something under 10% of the
total debt repaid. When you consider that in 2009 NFCC
member organizations helped to pay down nearly $2 billion in
consumer credit card debt, that's a lot of money. And the fact
is, the arrangement does benefit everyone: Consumers get out
of debt, creditors get paid back, and the counselors are able to
provide a vital service at a low cost.

FIVE SUPER-SIMPLE STEPS TO FINDING A GREAT NON-PROFIT CONSUMER CREDIT-COUNSELING AGENCY

> ### 1. Look for an agency that is a member of one of the major trade associations.

The best way to ensure that a non-profit credit-counseling
organization is truly trustworthy is to make sure it is affiliated with one of the two major credit-counseling trade associations, the National Foundation for Credit Counseling or
the Association of Independent Consumer Credit Counseling Agencies. Both of these organizations require counselors
to meet minimum training standards and adhere to a code
of ethical practices. Check with the organizations directly to
confirm whether an agency is in fact a member.

National Foundation for Credit Counseling
www.debtadvice.org
(800) 388-2227
Founded in 1951, the NFCC currently has about a hundred member agencies that assisted more than four million people in 2009. The counselors who work at NFCC member agencies must all go through what an NFCC spokesperson describes as a "grueling" certification process that involves passing six separate tests.

Association of Independent Consumer Credit Counseling Agencies
www.aiccca.org
(866) 703-8787
The AICCCA is much younger than the NFCC (it was founded in 1993) and it has only forty members, but according to its president, David Jones, these include many of the largest non-profit credit-counseling organizations. As a result, it, too, claims that its members served about four million people in 2009.

> ## 2. Ask the right questions
> ## when you first meet with them.

When you sit down and go through your initial counseling session with a non-profit credit counselor, you should ask the following questions.

- Are you a non-profit organization recognized by the IRS? (The answer must be yes, and they should provide you with proof.)

- What licenses do you have?

- How are your people trained and are they certified debt counselors?

- How long have you been doing this? What training do you have? (Many organizations have hundreds of employees doing the counseling; you want to work with someone who has experience and isn't a brand-new hire.)

- What is the counseling process like? How long will the first appointment take? What must I do to prepare?

- What happens after that? Will you provide a plan in writing for me?

- If you take over my bill-paying as part of a DMP, when exactly will you disburse payments to my creditors? (It should be at least twice a month.) Will you provide me with proof of payment and written progress reports? If so, how often?

- Will the money I send you as part of a DMP be protected and, if so, how?

- Do you offer any ongoing educational programs that will help me become smarter about getting and staying out of debt?

- What will counseling cost me—and will you put it in writing?

3. Interview more than one agency.

I'm a huge believer in the importance of doing your home-work. After all, you don't know what you don't know until you do. So before you sign up with anyone, make a point of interviewing at least two or three different agencies. In addition to learning about how they work, you want to see if the personal "chemistry" is right. This may seem like a lot of work, but it's important that you feel really comfortable and confident about the agency you select because you will likely be working with them for years.

4. Check out the agency with the Better Business Bureau.

Go to the Better Business Bureau website (**www.bbb.org**) and check to see if the agency you're considering is a member—and, if so, whether there have been any complaints filed against them. Even though I happen to know many excellent non-profit credit-counseling agencies that don't belong to the Better Business Bureau, I still think it's worth checking the BBB website. I would also Google the name of any agency you are considering along with the word "complaints" to see if anything comes up.

5. Get referrals and references.

Referrals from trusted sources are always a great way to go. So ask your friends and co-workers as well as any professionals you may work with (such as accountants or lawyers) if they happen to know of a GREAT non-profit credit-counseling organization in your area. The idea of asking about credit counseling may strike you as embarrassing, but it's time to stop being embarrassed and start taking action. If you can't get a personal referral, get the names of several agencies in your area from the NFCC or AICCCA—and then ask the agencies for references or testimonials from people like you whom they have helped. And then call those former clients and get their feedback on their experience.

Now that we've learned how the non-profit consumer credit counseling world works and what it can do for you, let's take a look at the "for profit" debt-reduction business, otherwise known as the debt settlement industry. As I said at the beginning of the book, this is a world filled with pitfalls, so it's important to know what to watch out for.

DEBT FREE FOR LIFE ACTION STEPS

- ❏ Decide if you're a good candidate for credit counseling.
- ❏ If you are, check with one of the two major trade associations for a member agency in your area.
- ❏ Come to your initial meeting prepared to question the counselor about his or her credentials, how he or she works, and what (if anything) the service will cost.
- ❏ Interview more than one agency, check them out with the Better Business Bureau, and ask for referrals and references.

CHAPTER THIRTEEN

DEBT SETTLEMENT: SOLUTION OR SCAM?

If it sounds too good to be true—it probably is too good to be true!

The debt-settlement industry has developed such a bad reputation that the full weight of the government is about to come down on it. As I write this, Congress is considering a consumer protection bill that would radically change the way this industry operates. In fact, by the time you read this, my guess is some form of legislation will have been enacted and the protections you deserve will be in place. But whether or not the government acts, you need to know the facts about what debt settlement is and what it isn't. So let's get started!

THE DEBT-SETTLEMENT GAME— WHAT YOU NEED TO KNOW

"Get Out of Debt with One Monthly Payment! Reduce Your Debt up to 50%!"

"Are you behind on your credit card bills, need cash to pay your debt off—call us, we can help you cut your debt in half in minutes!"

"New Government Programs! New free and easy programs are available for those who are in debt right now! Take advantage while they're still available!"

"If We Can't Get You Out Of Debt In 24 Hours, We'll Pay You $100!"

You've seen these ads, haven't you? Of course you have. They are everywhere—on television and radio, in newspapers and magazines, online in banner ads and mock advertorials. And the reason you and I are seeing these ads is because they are effective. People are calling.

But does any of what they promise actually work?

And what exactly are they promising?

According to the website of the industry's leading trade organization, The Association of Settlement Companies (also known as TASC), "Debt settlement companies act on behalf of consumer debtors to help them clear their debts. They do this by entering into direct negotiations with creditors in order to facilitate the repayment of debts."

In plain English, this means that they will pick up the phone and call a credit card company on your behalf. Say you owe $10,000 on your Citibank Visa and have fallen behind on your payments. The debt settlement company might call up Citibank and ask if they'd be willing to settle what you owe in return for an immediate cash payment of $5,000. Operating on the theory that something is usually better than nothing, Citibank would probably at least consider the offer.

Of course, if you're like most people who owe too much on their credit cards, you probably don't have $5,000 in cash to pay them. So in most cases the debt settlement company will suggest that you start sending them some money each month, which they will hold in a savings account. When the balance starts approaching $5,000, they will give the credit card company a call and see if they can make a deal.

Hmmmm. Doesn't this sound like something you could do yourself without having to pay anyone any fees or take any risk?

HOW DEBT SETTLEMENT OFTEN REALLY WORKS

Actually, the debt settlement strategy I just described is quite logical. But that doesn't mean it always works.

For starters, many creditors refuse to work with debt-settlement companies. So regardless of how good a debt-settlement company says it is, if you have debt with, say, American Express, Chase, or Discover Card, there won't be anything the company can do to help you. Why? Because as of this writing, American Express, Chase, and Discover have a blanket policy of not working with for-profit debt-settlement companies. As American Express spokeswoman Marina Hoffman Norville explained it, *"We believe there is no service or benefit that a for-profit debt-settlement company can offer our card members that they could not receive from working directly with us."* So before you even consider working with a debt-settlement company, it pays to check whether your credit card company will even talk to them.

On top of this, working with a debt-settlement company often creates immediate additional problems for you. Chances are that one of the first things they will suggest is that you stop making payments on the debt you're hoping to settle. If you ask why, they will offer what sound like two good reasons. For one thing, not paying your bills will allow you to send more money to them, which in turn will make your settlement fund grow more quickly. For another, as long as you continue to make payments, your creditor won't have any reason to settle your debt. Again, this is logical but not practical. The problem is that this approach can quickly destroy what's left of your financial life. Not paying a creditor you can afford to pay opens you to a world of hurt. The moment you fall behind on your payments, interest and penalty charges will begin to accrue, making your total debt even bigger. It will also immediately lower your credit score, which will make it even harder to refinance any of your debt. Even worse, many lenders routinely turn over debts that aren't being paid to collection agencies or attorneys, who may in turn sue you for payment.

The industry insists that reputable debt-settlement firms don't tell people to stop paying their bills, but countless reporters who have tested these claims have determined that they do. For example, NBC Today Investigates (the investigative unit on NBC's *Today* show) looked at one large debt-settlement company called Credit Solutions, which denied the complaint by a couple called the Wilsons that it had told them to stop paying their bills. In an effort to find out who was telling the truth, the *Today* reporter called the company pretending to be a potential client. "What do I do about my next credit card bill?" the reporter asked. "Do I go ahead and make that payment?"

"No, no—you stop right away," the Credit Solutions representative replied.

The *Today* report pointed out that even though Credit Solutions claimed a 99.5% customer-satisfaction record, the Better Business Bureau had received 1,600 complaints about the company in the previous three years and had given it a grade of "F." Moreover, after months of requests from NBC, Credit Solutions was able to come up with only one customer willing to provide a testimonial—this from a company claiming a 99.5% customer-satisfaction rate.

YOUR DEBT MAY ACTUALLY RISE

The fact is that even TASC admits that in most cases working with a debt-settlement company will cause your debt to increase. According to the trade association, a typical debt settlement client will see the amount he owes go up by an average of 20% over the two or three years that the settlement process generally takes. At the same time, as your debt falls increasingly past due, your credit score will suffer. And before too long, you may start getting anxiety-producing phone calls from collection agents.

TASC insists that if you stick with the program, the chances are good that all your debts will end up being settled for less than 50 cents on the dollar. There are lots of reasons not to believe this, and we'll get into that later, but even when a debt-settlement program works, it can still cause you trouble.

HURTING YOUR CREDIT SCORE— AND INCREASING YOUR TAX BILL

As I noted above, if you stop making payments on accounts, as many settlement firms suggest, your credit rating will immediately take a hit. According to FICO, stopping payments to creditors as part of a debt-settlement program can shave anywhere from 65 to 125 points from your credit score. What's more, if you wind up settling a debt for less than you owe, it will likely be reported to the credit bureaus not as "paid in full" or "paid as agreed" (both of which make you look good) but as "settled for less than full balance." Lenders hate to see this, and it will do terrible damage to your FICO score.

And once your debt is settled, that is *not* the end of it. A debt settlement is considered a negative event, and negative events stay on your credit report, affecting your credit score, for up to seven years.

Debt settlements also have tax implications. If you settle a debt to a financial institution like a bank or credit card company for less than you owe, the amount you don't have to pay (technically known as a "discharge of indebtedness") is considered taxable income—meaning you're going to wind up owing the government some money. And don't think you can just ignore this. The law requires creditors to report any and all debt reductions greater than $600 to the IRS.

IT'S NOT CHEAP AND THERE RARELY ARE REFUNDS

Finally, the debt-settlement process is not cheap. As a rule, the fee you're charged depends on the size of the debt you want the company to settle for you. TASC claims its members charge an average of 15% to 18% of a client's enrolled debt over three years, plus a service fee that might run $25 or $50 a month. (So if you're hoping to have them settle $10,000 in debt, you're probably looking at a total cost of around $2,000.) Keep in mind, though, that while TASC represents many of the biggest debt-settlement companies, it has only about 155 members in all, and many of the 1,000 or so companies that don't belong to TASC charge a lot more than TASC members do.

Many companies make you pay the fee in advance, and they generally keep it all whether or not they settle all your debts. There are a few debt-settlement firms that operate on a contingency basis, meaning you only have to pay if they come through for you, but they charge a much higher percentage— as much as 35% of the settled-debt amount.

Typically, at least part of the monthly payment you make to a debt-settlement company goes to pay your fee. Most firms will spread out the cost over a year or longer—deducting, say, $100 a month from your payment for 18 months. But some like to grab their entire portion up front. According to a 2010 report by the U.S. Government Accountability Office, known as the GAO, it's not unknown for clients to make sizable payments for as long as four months before a single cent is credited to their debt-settlement fund. Even worse, the files of the Federal Trade Commission and the Better Business Bureau are stuffed with accounts of desperate people who made payments for far longer than that—forking over tens of thousands of dollars in the process—and got nothing at all for their trouble except a ruined credit rating and even bigger debts than they started out with.

In one typical case cited by the GAO, a North Carolina couple, overwhelmed by credit card debt and desperate to avoid bankruptcy, agreed to pay a debt-settlement company $1,700 a month. Seven months later, having paid in more than $11,000, the wife called the company to check on where things stood. She was told they had accrued only $3,000 in savings and none of their credit card debts had been settled. The couple immediately withdrew from the program, but the damage was done. Since they had stopped making payments to their creditors, their total debt had ballooned, and they were now receiving collection notices and threats of lawsuits. In the end, they wound up having to declare bankruptcy.

In another case highlighted by the GAO, a single mother with small children in New York who owed $60,000 signed up with a debt-settlement company that told her all the advance fees she paid would be held in trust until all her debt was settled. Over the next several months, she paid the firm nearly $8,000. But then one of her creditors went to court and obtained a judgment against her, causing her bank account to be frozen. She telephoned the debt-settlement company to demand a refund, but her calls were never returned. She, too, wound up filing for bankruptcy.

A STRANGE DEFINITION OF SUCCESS

To hear the industry tell it, debt settlement almost always works. As many experts (including the GAO) have noted, Credit Solutions is hardly the only company that claims success rates of better than 90%. Of course, their definition of success is often downright strange.

Take this example reported by New York prosecutors. It involves a married couple whose credit card debt ballooned to almost $22,000 after the husband was laid off from his job. Desperate for help, the wife fell for a pitch from a telemarketer who told her that his company had checked out her family's credit history and believed that it could cut their credit card debt in half. So even though they were current on their bills, she and her husband joined the program and began making $325 in monthly payments to settle five accounts.

"Who wouldn't want to save 50% on their credit cards?" the wife told state attorneys.

Almost immediately, the debt-settlement company instructed the couple to stop paying their creditors, promising them that no penalties and interest would accrue as a result. That, of course, was totally untrue. Before long, they started getting harassing phone calls from their creditors at all times of day, including evenings and weekends.

Eventually, the company settled four of the couple's five credit card debts. Unfortunately, these only accounted for $3,000 of the $22,000 they owed. The remaining card company, to which they owed $19,000, refused to settle and instead went to court. In the end, the couple wound up having to repay the full $19,000—*plus* an additional $9,000 in penalties and interest.

Even though this outcome was (as the wife put it) "disastrous," the debt-settlement company sent the couple a "congratulations" letter, crowing about the fact that it had settled the $3,000 debt they owed their four small creditors for a little under $2,400. Talk about adding insult to injury! Not only was this a pretty pathetic saving, but when you count the $2,506 in fees the company charged them, the fact is that the couple didn't save a dime on the settled accounts. To the contrary, they wound up paying nearly $2,000 more than they originally owed.

As the wife pointed out, the debt-settlement company "failed our family in every respect, and we are counted as one of its success stories!"

Most outside observers peg the real success rate for debt-settlement programs at well below 50%, but even that may be optimistic. A recent study by the Colorado attorney general found that between 2006 and 2008 fewer than 10% of Colorado consumers who entered debt-settlement programs completed them successfully.

And the exaggerators are not just small, fly-by-night firms. In 2009, New York State attorney general Andrew Cuomo sued one of the nation's largest debt-settlement firms, Credit Solutions of America, a Dallas-based outfit that bills itself as the industry leader and claims to have helped 250,000 clients manage a total of $2.25 billion in debt. According to Cuomo, the company promised potential clients debt reductions of 60% or more; in fact, only about of 1% of its customers did anywhere near that well.

WHEN DEBT SETTLEMENT MIGHT MAKE SENSE

I noted earlier that by the time this book comes out, it's possible the entire debt settlement industry will have been shaken to its core. That's because there is a fast-growing group of legislators working with the FTC to put an end to the rip-offs. Specifically, they are considering new laws that would bar debt-settlement companies from collecting any fees from customers before they have actually settled any debts for them. If anything close to this winds up being enacted, the industry will be radically changed overnight.

So should you—or anyone—ever use a debt-settlement company? Personally, I wouldn't let anyone I love go this route. But there are some narrow circumstances when using one might make sense.

To begin with, debt settlement is something you should consider only if your debt problems mainly involve credit cards and other unsecured debt. If you're also struggling to keep the bank from foreclosing on your mortgage, you should concentrate on that. Saving your home is more important than paying off your credit cards.

Keep in mind, too, that whether you are doing the negotiating or some company is negotiating for you, certain kinds of debt are more likely to be settled than others. The best bets for settlement are:

- Debts owned by third parties. If your debt has been sold, the company that bought it almost certainly paid less than face value and will be highly motivated to settle.

- Debts that are so far past due that they are close to being written off by the lender.

USE THE DEBT-SETTLEMENT CHECKLIST

Here's a simple checklist you can use to help you decide whether debt settlement is right for you. If you can check off all of the boxes, the answer may be yes.

- ❏ I have sufficient income to pay my living expenses and still be able to repay at least 40% of my debt over the next three years.
- ❏ I have already tried negotiating my debts directly with the credit card issuer or other creditor without success.
- ❏ I understand that the process may not work and that my credit will be hurt.
- ❏ I am emotionally prepared to deal with creditors' phone calls.
- ❏ I have thoroughly checked out any debt-settlement company I am considering, including reading the Better Business Bureau report on it and talking to others who have used it.

FINDING THE RIGHT
DEBT-SETTLEMENT COMPANY

That last item in the checklist is crucial. The chances of running into a scam artist in the debt settlement industry are unfortunately very high, and you're asking for trouble if you don't check out a company thoroughly before you sign up with it.

What should you look for? For starters, go to the Better Business Bureau website (**www.bbb.org**) and run a search on the company you're considering. If you find they have hundreds of complaints and an "F" rating, then run from them. (This may sound obvious—but you'd be amazed how many people don't do this.) Next, check to see if the company belongs to TASC or the other big trade association USOBA (which stands for U.S. Organizations for Bankruptcy Alternatives). Both TASC and USOBA have an accreditation process and require their members to subscribe to an impressive-sounding code of ethics. I definitely would not recommend dealing with a company that doesn't belong to one of these organizations.

You can find out if a company belongs to TASC by visiting its website at **www.tascsite.org**. You can also call them toll-free at (888) 657-8272. Accredited members have been through a third-party audit of their procedures.

USOBA's website (**www.usoba.org**) does not list its members, but you can fill out a form to find out whether a company belongs.

Of course, just because a company belongs to either TASC or USOBA doesn't mean it's totally trustworthy. The names of more than a few TASC and USOBA members are among those listed in the GAO report as having ripped off unwary consumers. This is why you should also check with the Better Business Bureau and other consumer agencies to see whether a company you're considering has been the subject of complaints.

USOBA offers a number of helpful tips for finding a reputable debt-settlement provider. Among the highlights:

- A reputable company will always discuss the potential challenges as well as the benefits of their debt-settlement program before enrolling you as a client.

- A reputable company will not make claims about "Government Bailouts," "Obama Funds," "Consumer Stimulus Programs" or any other false claims about debt settlement being part of any government programs. (In fact, neither the Congress nor President Obama has created or endorsed any national debt relief plan for consumers that is offered by debt settlement companies.)

- A reputable company will provide a written explanation of its cancellation or refund policy.

- A reputable company will display the street address of its main office on its website.

- A reputable company will conduct a thorough review of your financial situation, including all expenses and income, before determining whether you are eligible for its debt-settlement program.

- A reputable company will provide you with a copy of its service agreement before asking you for banking information, accounting information, or your Social Security number.

Above all, you should shop around and compare. As USOBA points out, "There are a variety of Debt Settlement programs available and you should choose the one that makes the most sense for your particular situation." And as Ronald

Reagan used to say, "Trust, but verify." If a company tells you it belongs to or is affiliated with certain organizations, call the organizations to make sure.

FOR WHAT IT'S WORTH

All things being equal (which at this point they are, if you haven't yet started this process), I suggest that before you consider debt settlement, you first try my DOLP method or the DebtWise.com tools to get out of debt. If these approaches don't work for you, or you feel you need someone to help you with them, look for a non-profit credit-counseling organization.

Only after you've exhausted all these alternatives should you approach a debt-settlement company. And then make sure you do with your eyes wide open and your questions ready from the list I provided in this chapter.

Okay, my friend—we've made a ton of progress on your Debt Free For Life education and journey. Now let's take a look at an alternative that I personally regard as an absolute last resort, but something you need to know about anyway—the ins and outs of personal bankruptcy.

DEBT FREE FOR LIFE ACTION STEPS

❏ Use the Debt-Settlement Checklist to decide whether debt settlement is right for you.

❏ Make sure your creditors don't have a policy of refusing to deal with debt-settlement companies.

❏ Shop around, check with the Better Business Bureau, and ask for referrals and references.

❏ Before you turn over any personal information or sign any contracts, get a copy of the company's service agreement and cancellation or refund policy.

CHAPTER FOURTEEN

HOW BANKRUPTCY WORKS, WHEN TO USE IT, HOW LONG IT WILL TAKE YOU TO RECOVER

This is a chapter I hope you will never need to use. But even if you don't, you may know someone who isn't so lucky.

As I write this, estimates are that 1.6 million people will be forced to file for personal bankruptcy in 2010—twice as many as five years ago. Since the "great recession" started in 2008, not a week goes by that someone doesn't ask me, "David, should I declare bankruptcy?"

My answer is always the same: *If you think you may need to declare bankruptcy, get yourself some professional financial and legal advice TODAY.* The number-one complaint I hear from bankruptcy attorneys is that most people come to them too late—and as a result the attorneys are not able to protect any of their assets in court because they have already gone through all of them.

Most experts talk about bankruptcy as being a last resort, and I don't disagree. **BUT if bankruptcy is the right solution for you, the key to making it work is not waiting too long.** The sooner you get professional advice, the sooner the process can help you and the better off you will be. So with this in mind, let's look at what bankruptcy is, whom it can help, and whether or not it's right for you or someone you know.

WHAT EXACTLY IS BANKRUPTCY
AND HOW DOES IT WORK?

So what is bankruptcy? Technically, it's a legal declaration that you're unable to repay your creditors on time and in full. In practice, it is a way to wipe out many types of debt and give yourself a fresh start. The very act of filing a bankruptcy petition—that is, asking the bankruptcy court for protection under the federal bankruptcy statutes—immediately stops creditors from calling and gives you time to work things out by bringing at least a temporary halt to lawsuits, garnishments, repossessions, foreclosures, and evictions. (What happens is that the court appoints a trustee to oversee your bankruptcy, and the trustee informs your creditors that a filing has been made and that by law they can no longer bother you.)

If you complete the bankruptcy process successfully, all or part of your debts will be erased and your creditors will just have to write them off. It's truly legal magic. Once a bankruptcy court has declared a debt of yours discharged, it is gone, disappeared, eradicated—no one can legally make any attempt to make you pay it ever again. You don't even have to pay income taxes on the amount that's wiped out, the way you do when a debt is reduced in a debt settlement.

THE TWO CHAPTERS OF BANKRUPTCY
THAT YOU NEED TO KNOW ABOUT

There are several different types of bankruptcy, each named after a particular chapter in the federal bankruptcy code. Chapter 9 is for municipalities. Chapter 11 is primarily for businesses. Chapter 12 is for farmers and fishermen. **The two** chapters you need to know about—the ones for individuals—are Chapter 7 and Chapter 13.

CHAPTER 7

Chapter 7 absolves debtors of their obligation to repay most or all of their unsecured debts (such as credit card balances, payday loans, or medical bills). It is by far the most popular form of bankruptcy for individuals; it accounts for two-thirds of all personal bankruptcy filings. It is also the most severe form of personal bankruptcy—meant for people who owe so much and have so little that there's almost no chance they'll ever be able to pay what they owe.

Under Chapter 7, anything of value that you own except for some personal items and possibly some real estate can be taken and sold off by a court-appointed trustee to pay your creditors. Most Chapter 7 cases are simple. Debtors are required to attend a hearing with creditors and the bankruptcy trustee, but most never see a judge. If there's no controversy about your debts and assets, you're likely to complete the process and have your debts discharged in about four months.

CHAPTER 13

Chapter 13 allows a debtor to establish a court-supervised repayment plan. It is meant for people for whom repayment is a real possibility. They may just need a little extra time to make good on what they owe. It's also used by people who want to be able to keep assets they would not be allowed to keep in a Chapter 7 filing.

For the most part, you need a steady income to qualify for a Chapter 13 filing—which is why it is sometimes referred to as a wage-earner bankruptcy. Debtors who file for Chapter 13 bankruptcies are expected to work out a three- to five-year repayment plan under which some debts (such as child support) will be fully repaid, while others (such as credit cards) may be only partially repaid—or sometimes not paid at all. The plan must be approved by the bankruptcy judge, and once you've completed it, the court will officially erase whatever balances you still owe.

In fact, fewer than half the people who file Chapter 13 bankruptcies manage to complete their plans. This is because, with repayment plans spread out over so many years, there are lots of opportunities for something to go wrong, and it takes real discipline to stick to the plan.

BANKRUPTCY MAY BE RIGHT FOR YOU, BUT ARE YOU RIGHT FOR BANKRUPTCY?

In order to figure out whether declaring bankruptcy might make sense for you, you need to take into account a number of factors. Basically, it's appropriate to consider bankruptcy if your unsecured debts (such as what you owe from credit cards and medical bills) are so large that no matter how much you scrimp and save, there is no way you could repay them within five years. It also may be appropriate if you are behind on your mortgage or car loan and could use some extra time to catch up, but your lender is not willing to cut you any slack.

Of course, just because bankruptcy may look like a good solution to your debt problems doesn't mean it's the right solution for you. For one thing, there are a series of conditions you have to meet in order to qualify for bankruptcy protection. They include:

- **How much income you earn.** If you earn more than the median income in your state for families your size, you may not be allowed to file for Chapter 7 bankruptcy. Instead, the court may decide you can afford to repay some of your debts from future income and, rather than wiping out your debts right away, require you to enter a multiyear payment plan under Chapter 13.

- **What types of debts you owe.** Some debts cannot be discharged or reduced through bankruptcy. For example, bankruptcy won't help with child support or student loans and it cannot be used to reduce the amount owed on a first mortgage or a new or late-model car.

- **What kind of assets you own.** Many people are able to keep all their assets in bankruptcy. However, some assets are vulnerable, depending on the type of bankruptcy filing and where you live.

- **Your future outlook.** Will you be able to pay your bills on time once you emerge from the bankruptcy process? If not, you may want to delay filing. Why go through bankruptcy and then start running up new debts as soon as you get through it? If you think you're looking at more borrowing down the road, it's probably better to hold off on bankruptcy until you're in a position to discharge all your debts at the same time.

Let's look at all these factors in a little more detail.

HOW YOUR INCOME AFFECTS
YOUR BANKRUPTCY RIGHTS

As I noted earlier, you may not be allowed to file for Chapter 7 bankruptcy if you make too much money. Basically, if your monthly household income during the last six months before you filed is greater than the median income in your state for a family of your size, you will have to take a means test to see whether you qualify. The test is designed to calculate how much money you should be able to put toward debt repayment after subtracting some allowances for living expenses.

For example, as of this writing, the median income for a family of four in California happens to be $79,194 a year, or roughly $6,600 a month. So any family of four that earned more than $39,600 over the last six months would have to take the means test before being allowed to go the Chapter 7 route in California right now. If the test showed that they should be able to afford to pay off at least some of their unsecured debts, then the court would likely rule that the only way they could qualify for bankruptcy protection would be to file under Chapter 13 and agree to a repayment plan.*

This is important to know if you're considering bankruptcy and your income took a sharp drop within the last six months—say, because you just lost your job. In this situation, it might well make sense to delay filing until your six-month total reflects your current circumstances. For example, if you got laid off four months ago, waiting another two months to file would exclude the income you no longer have from the court's calculation.

---

* Keep in mind that even if your income is under the median, a court could still deny you the right to file Chapter 7 if it feels you earn enough to be able to pay at least some of your debts. As a practical matter, however, if you make less than the median, the odds are that you will be allowed to file Chapter 7.

You can find a version of the means test online at **www. legalconsumer.com/bankruptcy/means-test.** Median income information for your state and family size is available at **www. justice.gov/ust/eo/bapcpa/20100315/bci_data/median_ income_table.htm.**

WHAT KIND OF DEBTS
CAN BE WIPED OUT BY BANKRUPTCY?

For the most part, bankruptcy allows you to wipe out unsecured debt, such as credit card balances and what you owe from medical bills. And while it can't wipe out secured debt, it can often make it easier to manage.

As I explained earlier in the section about Debt Management Plans, a secured debt is a debt that is backed up (or guaranteed) by collateral, such as a mortgage secured by your house or a car loan secured by your vehicle. With this type of loan, the debt and the property go together, and bankruptcy can't separate them. If you want to get rid of the debt, you have to give up the property. Where bankruptcy can help you is when the property securing the debt is worth less than the amount you owe. This situation, known as being underwater or "upside-down" on the loan, has become increasingly common in recent years, particularly among homeowners who took out big mortgages to buy homes at the top of the market, only to see real estate values plunge. Often, when you're upside-down on a loan, simply giving up the property doesn't get you entirely off the hook. If the value of the property is less than what you owe, you've got to pay back the difference. Bankruptcy can be used to eliminate this obligation.

Bankruptcy can also be helpful with secured debt when you want to keep an asset. Say you're upside-down on a car loan, but feel you could afford to keep making payments if only the lender would lower your interest rate or give you more time to pay it off. If you're filing under Chapter 7, the threat of bankruptcy could improve your negotiating stance. After all, if you file Chapter 7 and the car is sold off, your lender will get only a portion of what he's owed—and because of your bankruptcy, he won't be able to collect the difference from you. Rather than run the risk of getting stuck like this, he might be willing to improve the terms of your loan if you agree to keep making payments.

If you're facing foreclosure, a Chapter 13 filing will bring the proceedings to a halt and give you time to catch up on missed mortgage payments. Chapter 13 can also transform some secured debt to unsecured debt, allowing it to be wiped out. Specifically, if you are upside-down on certain types of secured loans (mainly second mortgages and loans on cars that were purchased at least two and half years before you filed), the bankruptcy judge has the power to reclassify the debt. Say, for example, you have a $150,000 first mortgage and a $20,000 second mortgage on a house that is now worth only $140,000. The bankruptcy judge could rule that the second mortgage is really an unsecured loan—and like any other unsecured loan, it can be erased by bankruptcy. (The first mortgage, meanwhile, remains fully secured.)

WHAT KIND OF DEBTS CAN'T BE WIPED OUT

In addition to most secured debt, there are some types of unsecured debt that bankruptcy can't erase. These include:

- **Child support and alimony.** Filing for bankruptcy won't get you out of paying alimony or child support, which are classified as domestic-support obligations and thus have priority over other types of unpaid debts. That said, it is sometimes possible to reduce divorce-related property settlements through bankruptcy.

- **Student loans.** Although there is some support in Congress for legislation that would allow bankruptcy courts to wipe out private student loans (but not federally guaranteed ones), the general rule right now is that student loans cannot be discharged unless you can prove "undue hardship." Unfortunately, the law doesn't define "undue hardship." As a result, it's very difficult to predict whether a given individual will qualify for this break. It seems to depend mainly on the attitude of the bankruptcy judge and the experience level of your lawyer. The good news here is that there are administrative procedures separate from bankruptcy through which some student loans can be eliminated. (See Chapter Ten for details.)

- **Recent income taxes.** For the most part, bankruptcy will not discharge a tax obligation that is less than three years old. That said, payment of a recent tax debt may be stretched out through a Chapter 13 repayment plan. (If you can't afford even that, you may be able to settle a recent tax debt directly with the IRS through what is known as an "Offer in Compromise." See the IRS website at **www.irs.gov** for details.) Tax debts older than three years can be erased by bankruptcy, provided that the returns were filed accurately and on time. Late returns may be allowed if they were filed at least two years prior to the bankruptcy filing.

- **Legal judgments against you.** Generally speaking, bankruptcy will not wipe out debts incurred as a result of illegal behavior on your part. For example, drunk drivers who cause accidents in which someone is injured or killed can't escape the financial consequences of a legal judgment by filing for bankruptcy. Similarly, bankruptcy doesn't affect government fines and penalties, court-ordered restitution, debt related to theft or fraud, and debt related to intentional wrongdoing.

- **Some recently acquired debt.** Bankruptcy will not wipe out any cash advances of more than $875 within 70 days of filing and any debts to a single creditor for the purchase of luxury items or services worth more than $600 within 90 days of filing. It may seem like a clever tactic to run up big credit card balances just before you file for bankruptcy, but the law regards it as evidence of fraud—particularly if you've recently taken cash advances or spent money on travel or luxury goods and services. In general, bankruptcy won't help you if a creditor can make a good case that you incurred a debt with no intent or ability to repay it. For example, this might include debts you incurred after consulting with a bankruptcy attorney.

- **Any debts you don't list in your filing.** If you leave it out, it won't be discharged.

HOW MUCH OF YOUR STUFF WILL YOU HAVE TO GIVE UP?

One of the biggest—and most understandable—questions that people ask when they are facing bankruptcy is what it will mean in terms of losing the stuff they own. Will I have to sell my house and my car? What about my retirement accounts? My boat? My jewelry? The family heirlooms I inherited?

Basically, what you can keep and what you must give up when you file for bankruptcy depends on what kind of bankruptcy you're filing and whether the stuff you're worried about keeping is considered an "exempt asset."

I'll explain about exempt assets in a minute. The first thing you need to know about keeping your stuff is the difference between Chapter 7 and Chapter 13.

When you file for Chapter 7, the bankruptcy trustee appointed by the court has the right to sell off just about everything you own in order to raise money to pay off your creditors. Depending on where you live and how long you lived there, this may include your home and your car. The only things he can't sell are your exempt assets. The good news here is that because of exemptions and the low auction value of most used items, the trustee often takes nothing. But if you own any non-exempt asset that's worth more than a few thousand dollars, don't expect to be able to keep it.

Under Chapter 13, if you complete your payment plan, you can keep pretty much everything you own, no matter how much it's worth. But if you miss a payment or otherwise fail to complete the plan, the case could be converted to a Chapter 7 bankruptcy and your assets sold to pay creditors or your bankruptcy filing could simply be dismissed.

So what assets are exempt?

As I said, it depends on where you live. While federal bankruptcy law specifies what assets the federal government considers exempt, so do the laws of each of the 50 states—and they don't always agree. In fact, they vary widely. Under federal law, for example, a couple filing jointly may exempt a total of $32,300 in home equity. In other words, if their equity is worth more than that, the bankruptcy trustee could insist on selling their home in order to pay off their creditors. In contrast, both Florida and Texas place no dollar limit on home equity—meaning you can declare bankruptcy, have your debts wiped out, and still retain ownership of a multimillion-dollar house. (In fact, this has happened more than once.)

Whose definition do you use when federal and state law disagrees? Some 15 states leave it up to you to choose. But in the other 35, you have to use the state exemption. And just as there are huge differences between state and federal law on this score, so, too, are there big disparities from state to state. New Jersey, for example, exempts only $2,000 worth of household goods and other personal property (including your car), while Nevada will let you keep a total of $18,000 in personal property plus a $15,000 car. As the American Bar Association notes, "Similar variations among the states are found concerning a broad array of other exempt assets such as autos, jewelry, household furnishings, books and tools of the debtor's trade."

It stands to reason, then, that if you are contemplating filing for bankruptcy, one of the first things you want to do is find out what exemptions are available to you. You can find a summary of each state's bankruptcy exemptions at **www. legalconsumer.com/bankruptcy/laws/**.

YOUR RETIREMENT ACCOUNTS CAN BE PROTECTED—BUT NOT IF YOU'VE ALREADY CASHED THEM OUT

This is such an important point that I want you to read this section TWICE. In an effort to pay down their debts, many people in financial trouble pull money out of their retirement accounts before they meet with a non-profit credit counselor or bankruptcy attorney. Please don't do this. Filing for bankruptcy can protect your retirement accounts—but not if you already cashed them out! This is why I almost NEVER recommend cashing out retirement accounts to pay down credit card debts.

Regardless of where you live, your 401(k) and other tax-qualified retirement plans are typically protected in a bankruptcy. So are IRAs. The protection for traditional and Roth IRAs is capped at $1,171,650, but rollovers from retirement plans are allowed on top of the cap. Other types of assets that may be all or partly exempt include life insurance cash values, annuities, work tools, health and hearing aids, legal recoveries related to personal injury or wrongful death, and 529 college savings plans as well as income from Social Security, welfare, unemployment, alimony, or child support.

On the other hand, the bankruptcy trustee can claim tax refunds, refundable utility deposits, and vacation or leave-of-absence pay that you have coming to you.

WHY EVERYONE DOESN'T JUST MOVE TO TEXAS OR FLORIDA

Given the huge variation in state bankruptcy laws, you'd think anyone planning to file for bankruptcy would just up and move to Texas or Florida or some other generous state. The reason they don't is that lawmakers figured out this loophole and closed it up. Basically, if you've lived in a state for less than two years, you can't use its bankruptcy exemptions; you must use either the federal exemptions or those of the state you came from. What's more, if you've lived in a state for less than three and a half years, you can't get a homestead exemption of more than $146,450—even if it's a state like Florida or Texas that puts no limits on home equity. (If you live in a state where the homestead exemption is less than $146,540, then the lower state limit applies.)

If you're in this situation or you are thinking of moving, talk to a lawyer about your filing options. You may find it's worth your while to delay filing. You can find a quick summary of the rules regarding when you're entitled to claim a state's exemptions online at **www.exemptionsexpress.com.**

WHAT BANKRUPTCY WILL DO
TO YOUR CREDIT SCORE

Bankruptcy will definitely hurt your credit rating, but maybe not as much as you think. In fact, once you've gotten through it, you may find that you are more attractive to some lenders than you are now. This is partly because you will no longer be burdened by debt and partly because the law prohibits you from filing for another bankruptcy right away. (In the case of a Chapter 7 bankruptcy, you can't file again for at least eight years from the original filing date. For a Chapter 13, you have to wait at least two years after completing the payment plan.) As a result, if you can show that you've learned to handle your finances responsibly, you should be able to get credit again within a year or two of completing a bankruptcy.

Still, a Chapter 7 bankruptcy will stay on your credit report for 10 years; a Chapter 13 will continue to be listed for 7 years from the date of completion (for 10 years if you don't complete the plan). However, even while it's still on your report, the negative impact of the bankruptcy will gradually diminish because credit scoring gives the most weight to recent events.

Any debts discharged through bankruptcy should be listed on your credit report with a balance of zero. Check your report a few months after your discharge to be sure this has happened. If some debts still show a balance, dispute the report with the credit bureau. (See Chapter Eight for instructions on how to do this.) Note that bankruptcy will not erase a history of late payments from your credit report. You may not owe the money anymore, but your inability to pay on time remains a fact that nothing can change.

WHAT NOT TO DO

If you are thinking of filing for bankruptcy, there are certain things that can get you in trouble with the bankruptcy court. For example, failing to honestly disclose your assets, even if they are exempt assets, can result in your bankruptcy petition being thrown out by the judge without any of your debts being discharged. It could even result in criminal charges being filed against you. Other no-no's include transferring assets to friends or relatives for less than fair market value and paying off debts to family members or favored creditors.

Basically, anyone who thinks they can "game" the bankruptcy process is asking for trouble. You need to be totally honest about what you owe and what you have. As one legal expert told the *Los Angeles Times:* "The people that work in this field are very good at detecting an avoidance of the truth. There's a much better chance of being caught [cheating in a bankruptcy filing] than being caught cheating on your taxes." And if you are caught trying to get away with something, your bankruptcy will likely be canceled.

As I said at the beginning of this chapter, you also don't want to put off filing for too long. According to research conducted by the Consumer Bankruptcy Project (CBP), around 40% of those who file bankruptcy take at least two years to decide to pull the trigger—by which time many of them have exhausted most of their resources. "A lot of attorneys say they wish people would come earlier, before they emptied their retirement accounts or lost their car to repossession," researcher Katherine M. Porter told the *New York Times*. According to CBP lead researcher Elizabeth Warren of the Harvard Law School, waiting until your resources are entirely depleted defeats the main point of bankruptcy, "which is to help people rebuild their lives on a sounder footing" by protecting what they still have.

THE IMPORTANCE OF GETTING EXPERT HELP

Obviously, filing for bankruptcy is not something you should do without giving it considerable thought. Nor should you try to do it on your own.

Indeed, it is such a big step that the law requires you to complete two types of financial education before you will be granted a bankruptcy discharge. You must take a credit-counseling course sometime in the six months before you file and a personal financial management course after you file. The courses are provided by most non-profit credit-counseling agencies (see Chapter Twelve). They take about two hours, cost around $80, and can be done online. But make sure the provider you choose is approved by the Justice Department's U.S. Trustee Program. If it's not, you won't get credit for it. You can find a list of approved providers for your area online at **www.justice.gov/ust/eo/bapcpa/ccde/index.htm.**

TO LAWYER OR NOT TO LAWYER?

Although you need to be able to handle your financial affairs on your own, this doesn't mean that you should try to navigate the bankruptcy process by yourself. Bankruptcy law is so complex that if it is at all possible you should have an attorney experienced in bankruptcy cases to guide you through it. This is especially important if:

- You are considering filing Chapter 13.

- You have given a significant amount of money or repaid a debt to a friend or relative in the past year.

- You have a great deal of equity in a property that could be exempted, but the property is worth more than the exemption limit.

- You own property jointly purchased with a friend or relative other than your spouse.

- You have complicated financial affairs.

- You think you may have a good case for discharge of a student loan.

If you don't know anyone who can personally recommend a good bankruptcy lawyer, check with the following professional groups.

- **Non-profit credit counseling agencies.** These agencies all provide pre-bankruptcy counseling and can help you decide if you need to declare bankruptcy. If you do, they can help guide you to work with a bankruptcy attorney. (See Chapter Twelve to learn how to find a good non-profit credit-counseling agency.)

- **Bar associations.** The American Bar Association has a very useful referral site with many links (**www.findlegalhelp. org**). In addition, your state bar association website may include details on lawyers' specialties as well as disciplinary histories. Local bar associations also often offer information and referrals.

- **Legal aid organizations.** The websites of Legal Services Corp. (**www.lsc.gov**) and the American Bankruptcy Institute (**http://probono.abiworld.org**) both list organizations offering free help.

- **Advocacy and certification organizations.** The websites of the National Association of Consumer Bankruptcy Attorneys (**www.nacba.org**) and the American Board of Certification (**www.abcworld.org**) both have search functions designed to help you find attorneys in your area who are qualified to handle consumer bankruptcy.

- Online directories such as AVVO (**www.avvo.com**) include lawyer reviews.

It is possible to file a bankruptcy case without the help of a lawyer, particularly if it is a straightforward Chapter 7 case and you are certain you have a complete list of assets and debts. In this situation, instead of hiring a lawyer, you may be able to use a petition-filing service, which should charge only $200 or so to help you fill out all the forms. (By contrast, an attorney's fee for a routine Chapter 13 filing is likely to be in the neighborhood of $3,000.) A bankruptcy judge once told me that in a perfect world, everyone would be able to afford a lawyer, but since this isn't a perfect world, petition preparers perform a useful service, and the good ones can be a big help. Just keep in mind that they cannot give you legal advice.

BANKRUPTCY IS A TEMPORARY SOLUTION TO A TEMPORARY PROBLEM!

I want to end this discussion of bankruptcy with the following thought: Filing for bankruptcy is perfectly okay. It doesn't mean you're a failure or a terrible person. As I said before, well over a million people declare bankruptcy every year. If you choose to go this route, you will not be alone.

What I find really heart-wrenching is that there are people who have committed suicide rather than go bankrupt. NEVER, EVER let your financial situation convince you that life is not worth living. Bankruptcy is a TEMPORARY solution to a TEMPORARY problem.

The feeling of drowning in debt and not seeing any other way out but bankruptcy can drive a lot of people to the edge. Feeling desperate and depressed is not unusual. Just remember that as bad as things may seem, the fact remains that you can change your life. If you are feeling overwhelmed by your debts, please find a good credit-counseling agency and sign up today. And don't stop there. If you ever find yourself, even for a moment, considering hurting yourself, STOP and call someone you love. Tell them how you are feeling. If this isn't possible, then pick up a phone and call the National Suicide

Prevention Lifeline toll-free at (800) 273-8255 or visit their website at **www.suicidepreventionlifeline.org.**

Finally, and most important of all, remember these words: "This too shall pass." Believe me, it always does!

DEBT FREE FOR LIFE ACTION STEPS

❏ If you think bankruptcy might be the right solution for you, seek professional advice sooner rather than later.

❏ Take the means test online to see whether you would qualify for Chapter 7 bankruptcy.

❏ Understand what kind of debts would be wiped out by a bankruptcy—and what type wouldn't.

❏ NEVER raid your retirement accounts in an effort to stave off bankruptcy—get legal advice first!

❏ Get yourself expert help, including a credit-counseling course with a non-profit credit-counseling agency.

CHAPTER FIFTEEN

MAKE IT AUTOMATIC!
THE AUTOMATIC MILLIONAIRE 2.0

Getting out of debt—and staying debt free—requires commitment, discipline, and hard work. There are no shortcuts. But there is a way to make the job easier. It's something I've been writing, teaching, and talking about for years now. If you want to succeed, *YOU MUST MAKE YOUR PLAN AUTOMATIC.*

The single most important thing I've learned from working with hundreds of clients as a financial advisor, and now from coaching through my books and seminars, is that the only plans that work are the ones that are automatic! Discipline alone doesn't work. Simply working harder to save money usually doesn't work alone. Discipline and hard work take time, and if your plan requires hundreds of separate actions, month after month, year after year, it will fall by the wayside when the going gets tough. Sure, we'd all like to be prudent and disciplined and thrifty. But how many of us actually are? Over the years, I've had countless clients who insisted they were disciplined enough to do it themselves. In fact, there was only one who was actually able to stick to a financial plan manually (that is, by sitting down and writing himself checks every month) for any length of time.

The government knows we can't be trusted. That's why it came up with withholding to pay our income tax bill. It knows that the only way to guarantee that you will pay your tax bill is to take the money from your paycheck AUTOMATICALLY before you can spend it.

This is a strategy worth imitating. You need to do for yourself what the government did for itself: set up a system that guarantees you won't have spent all your money on other things before you get around to putting your hard-earned dollars where they are supposed to go—to ensuring a richer future. Set it up so that you only have to take action *once*, and you guarantee your success.

Even if you think you're the most disciplined person in the world, don't regard the automatic part as an optional extra. There is a reason it has its own chapter in this book. If you are serious about becoming Debt Free For Life, it's not enough to say you're going to do it. You've also got to make the process automatic.

If you follow the action steps in this chapter, you will truly have a foolproof, no-brainer, "set it and forget it" financial plan that, I promise you, will work. The plan is based on the one I laid out in my bestseller *The Automatic Millionaire*, but I've updated it for 2011. It will take you less than an hour to get it organized. Read the steps and follow the diagram. It's easy and, YES, YOU REALLY CAN DO IT.

Are you ready?

Then let's go make it automatic!

MAKING IT AUTOMATIC IN LESS THAN AN HOUR

1. Pay yourself first automatically.

In my books, TV and radio appearances, and seminars, I've always emphasized the critical importance of paying yourself first—having at least 5% of what you earn deducted from your paycheck and deposited directly into a 401(k), IRA, or similar qualified retirement account *before* the government takes its bite of withholding tax. Ideally, this deduction should total 12.5% of your income (the equivalent of one hour's worth of work each day). But whatever you can manage, you must make the process automatic. The good news is that payroll deduction is a standard feature of most 401(k) plans, so as long as you're signed up, your contributions will be automatically deducted from your paycheck.

If you're not eligible for a 401(k) or similar plan and as a result use an IRA for your retirement saving, you'll have to create your own automatic "pay yourself first" program. Tell the bank or brokerage where you have your IRA that you want to set up a *systematic investment plan*. This is a plan under which money is automatically transferred on a regular basis into your IRA from some other source (such as a payroll deduction). Most banks and brokerage firms will handle all the arrangements for you, contacting your employer's payroll department on your behalf and dealing with all the paperwork. (If your employer doesn't offer payroll deduction, you can have your retirement-plan contribution automatically moved from your checking account to your IRA—ideally, the day after your paycheck clears. Most banks have free online bill-paying services that allow you to schedule regular automatic payments of specified amounts to anyone you want.)

And yes, you should do this even if you are in debt! After more than two decades of experience teaching people about money, I have come to believe with all my heart that it's a big mistake to put off saving money until you are debt free. If you do, you may never get started saving. And you'll miss out on the matching contribution many employers offer on 401(k) plans. Instead, start by automatically saving a minimum of 5%—or the amount up to which your employer will match— and then gradually increase it to at least 10%.

2. Deposit your paycheck automatically.

If your employer uses a computerized payroll system, you should be able to arrange with your company's personnel or human resources department to have your pay automatically wired directly into your bank account. This is known as direct deposit. It gets your pay into your account without delay—and saves you the trouble of wasting a lunch hour every week or two waiting in line at the bank with a paper check.

3. Fund your emergency account automatically.

I've also long advocated the importance of maintaining an emergency cash cushion of at least three months' worth of expenses in an FDIC-insured bank account (*not* your regular checking account, but a separate one set up specially for this purpose). Until this emergency account is fully funded, you should have at least another 5% of your paycheck directly deposited into it. Again, if your employer doesn't offer payroll deduction, arrange to have your bank automatically transfer the money from your checking account the day after your paycheck clears.

4. Pay your credit card bills automatically.

Call all your credit card companies and arrange to have all your bills come due on the same day of the month—ideally, ten days after your paycheck is normally deposited. (Virtually every credit card company will work with you to change your due date if you ask them.) Then use your bank's online bill-paying service to automatically make the minimum payment for each of your cards five days before the bill is due. (If your bank doesn't offer free online bill-paying, think about switching to one that does.) If you want to pay more than the minimum on any of your cards—and if you follow my DOLP plan, you will—you can write a check for the extra amount. Making your minimum payments automatic ensures that you will never miss a payment deadline and get hit with late fees or penalty interest rates.

5. Fund your "extra payments" automatically.

In addition to making all your minimum payments automatically, you should also automate your "extra payments." Based on your DOLP plan or DebtWise.com "debt stacking tool," you now know which debt should be your #1 priority. If you add just an extra $10 a day to the minimum payment of your #1 debt, that's $300 a month that should be automatically added toward your debt each month. Arrange to have this amount (or whatever amount you've decided on) transferred automatically from your checking account to the appropriate loan account until it's paid off. Once you have automated this debt down to nothing, you should automate your #2 debt. And so on—until all of your debts are paid off completely. The same goes for your mortgage. If you add something extra to your mortgage payment, as I discussed in Chapter Nine, make that automatic, too!

6. Pay all your monthly bills automatically.

There are two kinds of monthly bills: regular ones that are always the same amount (like mortgage, rent, or car payments) and those where the balance due varies (like phone bills or electric bills or cable and Internet charges). You can automate payment of the bills that are a fixed cost by using your bank's online bill-paying service to have them automatically debited from your checking account each month. And you can automate payment of the variable ones by arranging to have them charged to one of your credit cards. As long as you keep your checking account adequately funded and you have sufficient credit available on your card accounts, this will protect you from ever missing a payment due date. My entire financial life is automated this way. As a result, all my bills are always paid on time, whether I am in town or not, and I never get hit with late fees or penalties.

You've now made your financial life automatic. Congratulations! You've taken a major step forward toward becoming Debt Free For Life!

DEBT FREE FOR LIFE ACTION STEPS

❏ Set up an automatic payroll deduction to fund your retirement account as well as other savings plans.
❏ Arrange for direct deposit of your paycheck.
❏ Use your bank's online bill-paying service to automatically take care of your monthly minimum credit card payments and other regular bills.

CHAPTER SIXTEEN

FIND THE MONEY! 7 SIMPLE WAYS TO FIND HUNDREDS OF DOLLARS (MAYBE THOUSANDS) IN LESS THAN AN HOUR

State treasurers and other government agencies are currently holding more than $32 billion in unclaimed assets from 117 million accounts that their owners have either forgotten about or never knew they had.

Now that you are motivated to get out of debt for good, I know you are going to want to look for extra money to add to your debt payments. With this in mind, I decided to write this chapter and share with you some tools that may help you "find the money"—money that you may already have but don't know about.

I assume that sentence above about the $32 billion in unclaimed assets got your attention. Well, it's true. Billions of dollars in unclaimed assets are sitting in government coffers—and maybe some of it is yours. So let's take a look. Who knows—you may find some money that's just sitting out there somewhere, waiting for you.

HOW I FIRST LEARNED ABOUT "FINDING THE MONEY"

I first learned about "finding the money" from the State Treasurer of Illinois, Judy Baar Topinka, whom I met a few years ago when I was speaking in Chicago at the Illinois Governor's Conference for Women. Over lunch before my presentation, I asked Ms. Topinka to share with me the favorite part of her job. She didn't hesitate. "I love helping people find money they don't realize they have," she said.

The comment baffled me, so I asked her what she meant. "When I took over this position, the state of Illinois was holding over a billion dollars in unclaimed assets," she said. She explained this was money from old bank accounts, 401(k) plans, insurance payouts, rebates, divorce settlements, tax refunds—you name it—that had gone unclaimed and was sitting in government coffers waiting to be found. "I have made a point of letting people in my state know about this," she said, "and as a result, we have been able to help thousands upon thousands of people find hundreds of millions of dollars they didn't realize they had left behind."

I told Ms. Topinka that I lived in New York, and she said, "Oh my. New York State has one of the biggest unclaimed money pots." When I got home I checked that out—and sure enough she was right. In New York State alone, officials are holding a reported *$9 billion* in unclaimed assets! I couldn't believe it.

$32 BILLION IN "ABANDONED" ASSETS ARE OUT THERE WAITING TO BE CLAIMED

That got me to thinking. If New York State has $9 billion in unclaimed assets, how big is the total treasure trove of cash nationwide?

The answer, I learned, is *very* big. According to the National Association of Unclaimed Property Administrators (NAUPA for short), as of 2010, treasurers and other officials in every state, plus the District of Columbia, Puerto Rico, and the U.S. Virgin Islands (as well as the Canadian provinces of Quebec, British Columbia, and Alberta), were sitting on at least $32.8 billion from some 117 million different accounts belonging to some 55 million people.

Now I have no idea if any of that money belongs to you, but don't you think it's worth taking a look? In 2006, $1.75 billion in unclaimed asserts was returned to the rightful owners of nearly 2 million abandoned accounts. That's an average of nearly $1,000 each. How great would it be to have an extra thousand dollars to put toward your Debt Free For Life Plan! So please read this chapter and go visit some of the sites I am about to share with you. Again, remember it's been reported that there are 55 million people in this country who have more than $32 billion in unclaimed assets just waiting for them. I call this FOUND MONEY. Imagine how much debt we could all pay off with that money?

Okay, enough said—let's go searching—and FIND YOUR MONEY.

Here's how.

---

1. Check the federal government's savings bond database.

According to the United States Treasury, more than $17 billion worth of Series E Savings Bonds have never been redeemed. These bonds were sold between 1941 and 1980, marketed by the government as a safe and patriotic way to invest. Maybe you got one as a gift. (I know I did—the dreaded "Grandma got you a savings bond" gift.) Apparently, a lot of recipients simply forgot about them.

There are more than 55 million savings bonds that people own, so it's not that much of a stretch to imagine that at one point maybe you were given a savings bond that you forgot to cash. Well, let's go and find out. You can do this in minutes.

Just visit the Treasury Department's savings bonds website (**www.savingsbonds.gov**) and navigate to a special page called TREASURY HUNT. (How in the world they were able to trademark "Treasury Hunt" is beyond me, but they are the government so they probably knew someone.) To get to the Treasury Hunt page, click on the tab for "Individuals," then on the tab for "Tools"—or just go to Google and search for the term "Treasury Hunt." The link is **www.savingsbonds.gov/ indiv/tools/tools_treasuryhunt.htm**.

Once you've reached the Treasury Hunt page, you'll find a big blue button two-thirds of the way down marked "Start Search." Click on it, type in your Social Security number, and you'll instantly be informed whether or not they are holding some bonds in your name!

If it turns out they are, you will need to fill out some forms to get your money back. Use form PD F 1048 if your savings bonds were lost, stolen, or destroyed; form PD F 3062-4 if your bonds never got delivered. Both can be downloaded from the Treasury Hunt page. Again, it's all FREE, and it can lead to FOUND MONEY!

---

2. Check the banks.

As much fun as it is to find money the Treasury is holding for you, it's equally fun to find money the banks may be holding for you. Remember that savings account you opened up with your parents as a kid? Did you every cash it out? What about the bank account you first opened up when you got married, or that college savings account your grandmother opened for your kids?

The fact is that people move, change jobs, get married, change their names, get divorced, change their names again, die—you name it. Every single day, money gets lost at the banks.

And it's not simply because people forget. These days, if there is no activity on a bank account for a year or so, the bank will send you a letter basically asking what's up and warning that if they don't hear back from you, they will consider the account to have been abandoned. Unfortunately, since one out of every seven Americans moves each year, these letters often don't reach the account holders and so their money goes into the unclaimed pile.

Here's how to find the money that you may have lost.

My first stop would be the NAUPA website, **www.unclaimed.org**, which provides links to the individual databases of all fifty states listing unclaimed assets. I'd also visit **www.missingmoney.com**, a one-stop-shop for finding unclaimed property that is operated by a private company for NAUPA.

What distinguishes both these websites is the huge amount of data they can access—and the fact that both of them are FREE. There are also unclaimed-asset sites that will charge you to do a search. A typical example is **www.unclaimed.com**. Its address is so similar to NAUPA's free site that you could easily get confused. Please go to the correct site, **www.unclaimed.org**. I'm recommending you take the FREE approach first! The other sites charge up to $18 per search.

3. Check with the FDIC.

Now I want you to go online and visit the FDIC website at **www.fdic.gov**. Not a week goes by that a bank somewhere in the United States isn't taken over by the Federal Deposit Insurance Corporation, or FDIC. The FDIC moves in to protect our savings when a bank is in danger of failing. In the process, it becomes responsible for all insured deposits and for liquidating any of the bank's remaining assets. Many of these assets are often unclaimed. If you can prove that an account belonging to you is among them, the FDIC will be more than happy to give you your money.

When an FDIC-insured bank fails and is liquidated, the FDIC's resolution division is responsible for paying:

- Unclaimed insured deposits up to the insurance limit

- Dividends declared on excess deposits over the insurance limit

- Dividends declared on general creditor claims

- Funds distributed to the shareholders of the failed institutions

According to the FDIC, there are several different reasons why these funds remain unclaimed, among them:

- An insured deposit wasn't claimed from the bank that took over the assets

- A dividend check on an excess deposit amount was not cashed

- A dividend check on a general credit claim was not cashed

- A check to the shareholder was not cashed

- A valid address is not on file and a dividend check was returned to the FDIC

So if you think you might have once had an account at a bank that was taken over by the FDIC, go online and visit the FDIC website at **www.fdic.gov**. At the top of the home page, click the tab labeled "Consumer Protection," and then the tab labeled "Banking & Your Money." This will take you to a page where you will see a list of links under the heading "Learn More." Click on the one that says "Search for Unclaimed Funds." (The direct link is **www2.fdic.gov/funds/index.asp**.)

Toward the bottom of the "Unclaimed Funds" page, you will find a search function you can use to see if there is an unclaimed account belonging to you in the FDIC's database. The only information you need to input is your name and the name of either the failed bank OR the city it was in OR the state it was in. Once you've done that, it will instantly tell you whether the database contains anything under your name. If it does, to claim your funds, you need to fill out an FDIC Claimant Verification Form. You can download the form from the Unclaimed Funds page. Then have it notarized and mail it to:

FDIC
Attn: Claims Department—Unclaimed Funds
1601 Bryan Street
Dallas, TX 75021

Be sure to have the FDIC reference number, which you will obtain from the online database. You should hear back from the FDIC within 30 days of filing your claim. If you have any problems with the process, you can email the FDIC directly through the **www.FDIC.gov** website.

4. Check the Pension Benefit Guaranty Corporation.

The Pension Benefit Guaranty Corporation, otherwise known as the PBGC, is a federal corporation that was created to protect the pension rights of the more than 44 million American workers and retirees who are enrolled in private employer defined benefit plans. As of 2007 (the most recent year for which data is available), the PBGC was holding more than $133 million in unclaimed pension benefits for 32,000 people!

I find this simply amazing. There are 32,000 people who worked at a company for years, earned themselves a pension, but never collected it! According to the PBGC, the average recipient on its unclaimed assets list is owed $4,950—but at least one account is worth $611,028!

If you're wondering whether it's worth your while to go to the PBGC website to see if you might have any missing pension benefits coming to you, here's a fact to consider: Over the last 12 years, more than 22,000 retirees have used it to collect $137 million in previously unclaimed benefits. I call that FOUND MONEY!

So if you or a relative of yours ever worked for a company with a Defined Benefit Plan (not a 401(k) plan), head right now to the PBGC website (**www.pbgc.gov**) and do a search to see if you have any unclaimed benefits coming to you. Here's how it works: On the home page, click on the tab labeled "Find Missing Participants" and follow the instructions to run a search. You should also download the PBGC booklet "How to Find a Lost Pension." In just 40 pages, it covers everything you need to know about searching for lost benefits. (You can also get this booklet for FREE by writing to PBGC Communications and Public Affairs Department, 1200 K St., NW, Washington DC 20005-4026.)

Here's an important tip from the PBGC that can save you from someday becoming a "missing participant": If you are or ever have been enrolled in a defined benefit plan, always keep your employer informed of your current address and any name change, even after you stop working for them. It is especially important that you continually let your former employers know whenever you move so they can always find you in the event you are owed a benefit.

---

5. Check with the IRS.

Am I really suggesting that you check with the IRS to see if they have any money for you?

YES, that's exactly what I'm suggesting—and, yes, I mean it.

Of all my recommendations, this is the one most likely to actually put money in your pocket. When we think of the IRS, most of us worry that we owe *them* money. But not everyone does. In fact, many of us are owed money, maybe you!

The place to go to find out is the IRS website at **www.irs. gov**. I absolutely LOVE this website. It is truly a treasure trove of FREE information that can help you get refunds you never collected, get tax credits you never realized you were eligible for—in short, get what you are owed.

You wouldn't believe how much money people who DON'T file their taxes are owed in refunds. You read that correctly. I'm talking about the government owing money to people who never bothered to file a tax return. It turns out that in an average year, non-filers fail to claim more than *$1 billion* in refunds! That's right—MORE THAN ONE BILLION

DOLLARS in uncollected refunds is just sitting at the IRS not going anywhere because the taxpayers who are entitled to the money didn't file returns.

Why would someone not file a return? There are all kinds of reasons, but usually it's because they couldn't be bothered or because they think their income is so low that they don't owe taxes (not realizing that because of withholding they may be entitled to a refund). Whatever the reason, the IRS estimates that for the 2006 tax year, there were roughly 1.4 million people who fell into this category—and who, as a result, are owed more than $1.3 billion. That's more than $900 per person!

Now here's the big catch. The IRS has a rule that you have to claim your refund within three years from the time your return was due or they get to keep the money. By the time this book goes on sale, it will likely be too late for anyone to claim a refund for 2006. But if you have a refund coming to you for 2007 or later, you still have a chance to get your money.

Check out the table below, which I got from the IRS website. It breaks down uncollected refunds by state. They know exactly how many people in each state they owe money to! Could you be one of them?

INDIVIDUALS WHO DID NOT FILE A 2006 RETURN WITH AN ESTIMATED REFUND			
	Individuals	Median Estimated Refund	Total Estimated Refunds ($000)*
Alabama	21,800	$608	$18,839
Alaska	6,300	$693	$6,997
Arizona	39,900	$507	$33,921

Arkansas	11,800	$579	$10,543
California	159,700	$554	$150,640
Colorado	25,200	$531	$23,119
Connecticut	15,500	$686	$18,676
Delaware	5,200	$622	$5,297
District of Columbia	5,100	$601	$5,448
Florida	101,700	$641	$110,709
Georgia	45,700	$560	$42,642
Hawaii	9,500	$668	$10,658
Idaho	5,800	$482	$4,723
Illinois	51,400	$655	$54,740
Indiana	26,600	$641	$24,146
Iowa	12,200	$596	$9,990
Kansas	13,400	$586	$11,771
Kentucky	14,500	$610	$12,976
Louisiana	23,800	$641	$24,615
Maine	4,900	$561	$4,203
Maryland	30,800	$616	$29,938
Massachusetts	29,000	$669	$31,939
Michigan	42,800	$618	$40,790
Minnesota	18,900	$552	$16,227
Mississippi	11,800	$567	$10,120
Missouri	25,800	$561	$21,090

Montana	4,000	$530	$3,425
Nebraska	6,100	$590	$5,390
Nevada	19,400	$575	$19,163
New Hampshire	5,400	$706	$5,943
New Jersey	39,900	$666	$43,030
New Mexico	9,800	$560	$8,612
New York	76,700	$666	$87,563
North Carolina	39,100	$539	$32,919
North Dakota	2,100	$589	$1,875
Ohio	44,600	$593	$38,467
Oklahoma	18,200	$576	$15,779
Oregon	21,900	$490	$18,340
Pennsylvania	47,100	$652	$45,050
Rhode Island	4,300	$652	$4,231
South Carolina	16,400	$534	$13,810
South Dakota	2,500	$604	$2,193
Tennessee	22,200	$598	$19,756
Texas	109,600	$653	$114,720
Utah	9,200	$528	$9,592
Vermont	2,200	$565	$1,782
Virginia	40,600	$594	$39,460
Washington	37,100	$641	$39,713
West Virginia	4,800	$660	$4,775

Wisconsin	17,000	$564	$14,903
Wyoming	2,900	$691	$3,229
US Armed Forces	4,800	$821	$4,367
US Possessions & Territories	200	$887	$444
Totals	1,367,200	$604	$1,333,288

*Excluding the Earned Income Tax Credit and other credits.

Source: www.IRS.gov

BUT WAIT—THERE'S MORE AT THE IRS

It's not just non-filers who don't get their refunds. A lot of refunds go undelivered each year to people who did file. How many? In 2008 (the most recent year for which figures are available), nearly 102,000 taxpayers who filed tax returns and were supposed to receive a total of $123.5 million in refunds never got their checks.

What do you do if you're one of those taxpayers? It's simple. You go online to the IRS website (**www.irs.gov**) and you click on the link labeled "Where's My Refund?" You then input some basic information about yourself (Social Security number, filing status, and the amount of refund you're due) and the site will tell you the status of your refund. If you don't have access to the Internet, you can phone the IRS toll-free at (800) 829-1040 and ask them if they're holding a tax refund for you.

Since 2004, taxpayers have used the "Where's My Refund?" tool more than 24 million times. If you think there's even a remote chance that you never got a refund you were supposed to get, you should join this crowd.

How come all those people never got their checks? Usually, it's because they moved and the IRS didn't have their new address. So how many times have you moved in the last few years? Are you sure the IRS has your current address? Don't assume they know where you are. You want to be sure they have your correct address.

The way to do this is to file a change-of-address form (Form 8822), which you can download from the IRS website. You can also call the IRS directly at 1-800-TAX-FORM (800-829-3676) and ask them to send you one.

I filed an 8822 form myself this year; having moved three times in the last four years, I didn't want to take any chances that a refund I was due might go astray.

6. Check with Social Security.

One of the most important bits of advice I offer people is that it's critical to double-check the Social Security benefit statement you receive each year. You want to make sure that the earnings listed on the statement match what you actually earned.

You can check your statement online right now by going to the Social Security Administration's website at **www.ssa.gov.** Or you can call them toll-free at (800) 722-1213 and ask them to mail you your Social Security benefit statement. You are supposed to receive this each year, but if you have moved, it may be going to your old place. So, as with the IRS, make sure the Social Security office has your current address.

Over the years, I have found two mistakes on my own Social Security records. So trust me—it is worth taking the time to check. When you retire, the Social Security payments you receive will be based on what the SSA's records say you earned while you were working. If those records say your income was lower than it really was, your benefits will be lower than they should be.

NOW MAKE SURE YOU AREN'T MISSING ANY SOCIAL SECURITY CHECKS

Here's another one that baffles me. It's reported that approximately *half a billion dollars* in Social Security checks are either not deposited each year or otherwise go unclaimed. Again, much of this is a result of people moving and not sending the Social Security Administration their new address. But sometimes it's a result of ignorance. For example, when a spouse or parent passes away, the heirs often don't realize they may be entitled to benefits.

The Social Security Administration recommends that you touch base with them as soon as a family member passes away to make sure you receive all the benefits you are entitled to.

Here's an example of one of the many benefits that may be available:

A surviving spouse is entitled to a one-time payment of $255 if she or he was living with the deceased or, if living apart, was receiving certain Social Security benefits. If there is no surviving spouse, the payment is made to a child who is eligible for benefits on the deceased's records in the month of death.

Family members who may be eligible to receive monthly benefits include:

- A widow or widower age 60 or older (age 50 or older if disabled)

- A surviving spouse at any age who is caring for a child of the deceased who is under age 16 or disabled

- An unmarried child of the deceased who is younger than 18, or is 18 or 19 and a full-time student in an elementary or secondary school, or has a disability that began before age 22

- Parents, age 62 or older, who were dependent on the deceased for at least half of their support

- A surviving divorced spouse, under certain circumstances

Did you read that list carefully? Honestly, I don't think everyone knows about all of these Social Security benefits. Did you? Please make sure that you protect your family and those you love with this information. For some people, getting these benefits could change their lives!

Again, the place to go to get this information is the Social Security Administration's website at **www.ssa.gov**. Or call Social Security at (800) 772-1213.

7. Check for unused gift cards and gift certificates.

How many times have you received a gift card and never bothered to use it or used only part of it—or just flat out lost it? I know I do that all the time. And so do a lot of people. Indeed, according to the *Wall Street Journal* and research by Tower-Group, each year Americans spend about $65 billion in gift cards but don't redeem $6.8 billion.

Here's the good news. Depending on where you live, state law may require that unused gift cards and gift certificates with expiration dates or services fees must be turned over as unclaimed property.

In most cases, if you are given a gift card or certificate with a specific date, the unused balance is presumed abandoned five years from date of purchase. If the gift card is rechargeable, depending on the state, it may be considered abandoned five years from the date of the last owner-initiated transaction. Of course, each state has its own laws for unclaimed gift cards and its own system for finding these unclaimed assets. So your best bet is to first to Google the state treasurer's office in your state. Once you've arrived at their website, navigate to their unclaimed assets department and see if they have an area where you can search for abandoned gift cards.

A great example of what I'm talking about here is the State of Illinois' Treasury website. Remember I told you how I originally learned about unclaimed assets from the Illinois state treasurer? Well, her office has a website with an area called "CASH DASH" that lays out exactly how people in Illinois can reclaim these assets. Chances are that your state has something similar—so go and look.

By the way, retailers hate me telling you this. Many national chains have gone out of their way to move their gift-certificate business to states that haven't yet created laws to protect consumers from losing money on unused or expired gift cards. *Consumer Reports* regards this issue as so important that they launched a public education campaign about the pitfalls associated with gift cards, using the headline: "Last year, shoppers like you were out $8 billion because of unused, lost or expired gift cards . . ." Hard to believe—but all true, so go and take a look and find some of your money today!

DEBT FREE FOR LIFE SUCCESS STORY

David, I read many of your books. *Start Late, Finish Rich* gave me my first financial epiphany and got me to take charge of my financial life. Since reading it, I have paid off over $60,000 in debt and I expect to have my last credit card paid off by next June. *Go Green, Live Rich* helped me to decrease my utility bills by 25%. And an unexpected surprise occurred when I read *Start Over, Finish Rich*—which I did in one sitting. When I was reading about states holding unclaimed assets, I immediately put the book down, picked up my laptop and quickly checked the different states I had lived in. Imagine my surprise when I found $76.43 that the State of Colorado held for me! I feel incredibly happy and excited about my future now that I have a firm grasp on my finances. Thank you so much!

Jane J.
Fort Bragg, CA

PLEASE TELL ME IF YOU FOUND SOME MONEY!

Okay, now that you've learned the secrets to finding lost or forgotten money that may be yours, you have no excuse not to go out and start looking.

Honestly, the favorite part of my day is reading the success stories that readers send to me. If you wind up finding some money you never knew you had, please head over to **www. facebook.com/davidbach** and post what happened or send us a video clip. You can also email me at **success@finishrich. com** and let me know what happened. Your success story may inspire someone else to try this!

DEBT FREE FOR LIFE ACTION STEPS

❏ Check the federal government's savings bond database to see if you own any U.S. Savings Bonds you've forgotten about.

❏ Visit **www.unclaimed.org, www.missingmoney. com**, and **www.fdic.gov** to see if any banks or government agencies are holding any unclaimed assets for you.

❏ Visit **www.pbgc.gov** and **www.ssa.gov** to see if you have any unclaimed pension or Social Security benefits coming to you.

❏ And don't forget to check with the IRS to see if they might be holding an unclaimed refund for you.

❏ Check your wallet or purse for any unused gift cards or gift certificates.

A FINAL WORD

FROM IN DEBT TO DEBT FREE—
AND A DREAM TRIP—ALL IN LESS THAN A YEAR

As I was finishing up this book, I received an email from a reader named Farren. Farren was in the middle of taking my FinishRich Coaching Program, and he was writing to let me know that even though he hadn't yet finished the course, his entire life had already completely changed. In less than eight months, he had gone from being stressed out over his finances to being out of credit card debt and on his way to a dream trip—seven weeks in Australia with his wife and two young sons.

As I read his email, it really hit me—it's all about mindset and action. Farren's mindset had changed, and as a result so had his actions.

Here's the original email Farren sent me. I want you to read it because there's so much in it to learn from. The fact is, you too can enjoy this type of success.

David, I just wanted to send a quick email to thank you once again for providing a great product/service and resource. I have listened to the CDs, watched the DVDs, read your book "Start Over, Finish Rich," implemented the strategies, and changed my mindset!

In less than a year, we've paid off $12,000 in American Express credit card debt, drastically reduced our monthly ex-

penses, created a financial future with less stress, and—drum roll, please—the most exciting thing is that we are taking 7 weeks off for a family trip to Australia! (And I was able to pay cash for the $6k airfare!) My wife and two boys age 5 and 8 years old are so excited.

I took a picture of our little home savings jar that we used as a visual reminder for our kids and ourselves to see what we were saving for and how much we were saving. My kids are now excited to save. When they find a nickel or a penny—even change in my car—they run to the kitchen to put money into our "Australia Fund."

Really life-changing stuff . . . so thanks to you and your team for their financial wisdom. These are troubled times for some, but with a plan and a coach, there's nothing stopping you from the greatest life change you can do . . . understanding how to be financially free!

Cheers to you guys and "hi 5"! Thanks again!

Live your dream,

Farren West

I wrote back to Farren immediately, telling him how amazing I thought his email was. It was as if he had just read *Debt Free For Life*. "I love how you changed your mindset, took action and involved your family!" I wrote him. "You are an amazing example of how quickly you can get out of debt and start LIVING YOUR DREAMS. Nearly two months in Australia—sounds incredible!"

Farren's response was as inspiring as his first note:

We have just barely implemented your systems and still have made significant changes and progress. But it's really like you said—it's all about mindset and action. If you are married, you

really have to have a "come to Jesus" meeting with your signifi-
cant other. Look at ways you are both wasting money, create
a goal, and go after it. A visual reminder like the jar in our
kitchen also really helps. And if you can get the kids involved
and excited, that can make all of the difference.

YOU COULD BE THE NEXT GREAT SUCCESS STORY!

Farren's story touches me for many reasons—and maybe it touches you, too.

First, even though Farren was in debt, he was still will-ing to invest in himself to learn more about handling money and building wealth. With the benefit of what he learned, he changed his mindset and he took action. He'd didn't over-think it—he just got going. He also involved his whole family in his dream of being debt free. He sat down with his wife and had the hard talk about looking for ways to cut back on spending. Then they created a visual aid (the money jar) to help them save money—and they got their kids to participate. As a result of all this, in just eight months, Farren was able to pay off a $12,000 credit card debt—and on top of that save enough to be able to pay cash for $6,000 in plane tickets and take his family on a two-month dream trip to Australia.

I mean, really—it's a story that can make you jealous. Here's a couple in debt, struggling to keep their heads above water, and in less than a year their whole life is turned around—sim-ply as a result of changing their mindset and taking action (plus a little bit of coaching and education).

There is another thing about Farren's story that really touched me. When I received his email, I was staying at a very nice hotel in Del Mar, California, where I wrote a lot of this book. That particular day I happened to be having lunch with a close friend who is very well off. My friend was telling me how he hoped he could make enough money over the next four years to be able to take six months off. Now, my friend is worth at least a few million dollars, so I said to him, "Steve, you could take that time off now. Look at this email I just got. This guy was up to his eyeballs in credit card debt six months ago, and now he's paid it off and figured out how to take seven weeks off. If this guy can pull this off in less than a year, there's no reason you need to wait four years to go for your dream."

My friend read Farren's email—and it immediately got him thinking. He looked up at me and said, "You're so right. It really *is* all about mindset. Maybe I *can* do this sooner than four years." He shook his head and laughed. "When your book is done, send it to me," he added. "I need to read it."

IF FARREN CAN DO IT, WHY CAN'T YOU?

So now back to you! I really hope this book has given you the tools and the mindset you need to take action to live DEBT FREE FOR LIFE. Stories from readers like Farren are why I keep doing what I do—and I hope that if you achieve success, you, too, will share your story with me. You can email me at **success@finishrich.com** or through our website at **www.finishrich.com** or **www.facebook.com/davidbach**. Who knows, I might surprise you and write back to you right away.

Real success stories from real people are incredibly compelling. When you read stories like Farren's, part of you has to think, "Why not me? If they can do this, why can't I?" That's simply how our brains work. Most of us have a competitive instinct that says, "If he can do that, so can I." That's your gut speaking to you. And trust me when I tell you that your gut is right!

There are literally thousands of success stories on our website. Take a few minutes to read through some of them. I'll bet they leave you feeling even more motivated to take action than you already are.

SO NOW GET GOING

> *"The way to get started is to quit talking and begin doing."*
> —**Walt Disney**

I really can't think of a better quote with which to end this book—and for you to begin your journey toward being Debt Free For Life—than these words by Walt Disney. Ironically, as I type these final paragraphs, I'm getting ready to take my son Jack to Disneyland for his seventh birthday tomorrow. Disney was a dreamer. He was turned down by hundreds of banks, and it took him years to make his dream come true. But he was also more than a dreamer. He was a "doer" too. And thanks to his doing, his dream became a reality—one that the world has been enjoying for generations.

Now consider your dream. What is it? It doesn't need to be as big as building Disneyland. Your dream may simply be to be able to pay off your credit card debts over the next few years. Well, understand this—it can be done. You now have the tools to do it. Whether you use my DOLP system or the DebtWise.com website, you've got the tools you need to prioritize your debt and calculate your "Debt Freedom Day."

Have you visited **www.DebtWise.com** yet? You can create

a customized plan to get yourself out of debt in less than 10 minutes. So what are you waiting for? Go do it now! Remember, because you bought this book, you're entitled to a free trial of DebtWise.com. Why not take advantage of it?

What about your mortgage? Did my tips on how to pay off your mortgage early inspire you to change how you make your payments (either by starting a bi-weekly plan or adding an extra month's payment at the end of each year)? Well, then, get going!

Student loans got you down? Did you use the information I gave you to make better decisions on paying it down faster? How about the interest on those credit cards you have? Did you use the tools in the book to lower your rate as I suggested? Did you pick up the phone and try to negotiate a better deal? Did you give up after one call or did you keep trying?

Maybe you liked the idea of getting a trained counselor to guide you out of debt—and maybe help you set up a Debt Management Plan. If so, did you do something about it—or are you still waiting? *Don't wait any longer.*

Maybe you were surprised by how easy it is to make your financial life AUTOMATIC. Did you read my plan and think, "This is really simple! I could do this!" So *did* you do it? If not, get doing.

And how about all those great websites I listed where you can go to "find your money"? Have you checked any of them out to see if there's money of yours sitting in some government account somewhere? What have you got to lose? Every day I get emails from people who have found money using these free sites. *Go try them.* You've got a much better chance of finding some lost money that belongs to you than you have of winning the lottery. So spend an hour searching.

In the end, whichever part of the DEBT FREE FOR LIFE

program got you excited, there is one question I want you to ask yourself right now.

Why not?

WHY NOT YOU? RIGHT NOW—START TODAY!

Why not you? Right now! Why not be one of the many people who will read this book and DECIDE today to begin DOING? You are ready to act. You now have so much knowledge about debt that you could actually start helping others. But first, help yourself! If you try one of my suggestions and you don't like the results, you can always go back to what you were doing before.

The truth is I don't think you will ever go back. Very few people who truly DECIDE to be debt free change their minds later on and decide that they liked being in debt better. I started this book talking about our grandparents and great-grandparents who survived and ultimately thrived following the Great Depression. Think back on them now. I know my grandparents didn't change their mind about freeing themselves from debt. My grandmother Rose decided to be debt free—and she died debt free, a millionaire. She passed her knowledge of being debt free and investing to her family, and she shaped not just her destiny but that of her children, grandchildren, and great-grandchildren.

Why not you? *Why not start today?* **You could change your destiny today.** I truly believe you will be happier with less debt—and I know that in just three to five years, if you follow the systems I have laid out in this book, your entire financial life will be better. You'll have less stress—and you'll probably be healthier too. One interesting thing I've noticed is that many of my readers who lose debt also lose weight. Remember Nicole's success story back in Chapter One? Whenever she thinks about spending money on a snack, she now asks herself, "Is this purchase really necessary?" As a result, she has saved more than $6,000 in six months—and lost 21 pounds! Cool story—right? Why not you?

BET ON YOURSELF TO WIN—
AND ENJOY THE JOURNEY

In truth, the DEBT FREE FOR LIFE process isn't just about the result—it's also about the journey. As soon as you start working on paying down your debt, you will begin to feel better. As you see yourself making progress, each day will seem a little freer, a little less stressful, a little more joyful.

I know you bought this book and took the time to read it because you are special. Because you believe in yourself. People who are cynical or pessimistic generally don't buy books about having a better life. They simply say, "That won't work for me" and move on.

That's not you. You believe in yourself. And you should. Tom Hanks, the Oscar-winning actor, once said something that changed my life forever. He was asked what he regarded as the best part of his success. Now, Tom Hanks has won so many awards, starred in so many successful movies, had such an amazing career. But out of all that, what do you think he identified as his greatest accomplishment? He said it was that although a lot of people didn't believe he could do it, he *did* believe. And not only did he believe, but he decided to bet on himself to win. And guess what? It worked!

Just typing that gives me shivers. Around the time I heard

Hanks say that, I had a dream of my own. It was to write a book called *Smart Women Finish Rich*. Just about everyone told me it was a dumb idea—and I shouldn't do it. You now hold my twelfth book in your hands (a book, by the way, that took me five years to convince my publisher to let me do). At the end of the day, I "bet on myself to win"—and that has made all the difference in my life.

Like Tom Hanks, I say, "Bet on yourself to win!" If that's the only thing you get from this book, then reading it was worth it. There really is no greater gift than this realization. And you deserve it.

So good luck on your journey. And please email me at **success@finishrich.com** if this book touches you or changes your life for the better. Also, please join our community at **www.finishrich.com** or **www.facebook.com/davidbach** so we can keep in touch. Almost every day on my website I post new information that can help you live and finish rich.

Until we meet again, enjoy the sweetness of your life and, truly, enjoy the journey!

Make this life of yours special—because it is.

Your friend,
David Bach

INDEX

ABOUT THE AUTHOR

David Bach has helped millions of people around the world take action to live and finish rich. He is one of the most popular and prolific financial authors of our time, with ten consecutive national bestsellers, including two consecutive #1 *New York Times* bestsellers, *Start Late, Finish Rich* and *The Automatic Millionaire*, as well as the national and international bestsellers *Start Over, Finish Rich; Fight for Your Money; Go Green, Live Rich; The Automatic Millionaire Homeowner; Smart Women Finish Rich; Smart Couples Finish Rich; The Finish Rich Workbook*; and *The Automatic Millionaire Workbook*. Bach carries the unique distinction of having had four of his books appear simultaneously on the *Wall Street Journal, BusinessWeek,* and *USA Today* bestseller lists. In addition, four of Bach's books were named to *USA Today's* Best Sellers of the Year list for 2004. In all, his FinishRich Books have been published in more than 15 languages, with more than 7 million copies in print worldwide.

Bach's breakout book, *The Automatic Millionaire*, was the #1 business book of 2004, according to *BusinessWeek*. It spent thirty-one weeks on the *New York Times* bestseller list and was simultaneously number one on the bestseller lists of the *New York Times, Business-Week, USA Today,* and the *Wall Street Journal*. With more than a million copies in print, this simple and powerful book has been translated into 12 languages and has inspired thousands around the world to save money automatically.

Bach is regularly featured in the media. He is a regular contributor to NBC's *Today* and appears on its popular weekly "Money 911" segments. He has appeared six times on *The Oprah Winfrey Show* to share his strategies for living and finishing and has made regular appearances on NBC's *Today* and *Weekend Today* shows, CNN's *Larry King Live*, ABC's *Live with Regis and Kelly*, *The View*, CBS's *Early Show*, ABC News, Fox News, and CNBC. He has been profiled in many major publications, including the *New York Times*, *BusinessWeek*, *USA Today*, *People*, *Reader's Digest*, *Time*, *Financial Times*, the *Washington Post*, the *Wall Street Journal*, the *Los Angeles Times*, the *San Francisco Chronicle*, *Working Woman*, *Glamour*, *Family Circle*, and *Redbook*. He has been a contributor to *Redbook* magazine, *Smart Money* magazine, Yahoo! Finance, AOL Money, and Oprah.com.

David Bach is the creator of the FinishRich® Seminar series, which highlights his quick and easy-to-follow financial strategies. In just the last few years, more than half a million people have learned how to take financial action to live a life in line with their values by attending his Smart Women Finish Rich®, Smart Couples Finish Rich®, and Find the Money Seminars, which have been taught in more than 2,000 cities throughout North America by thousands of financial advisors.

An internationally renowned motivational and financial speaker, Bach regularly presents seminars for and delivers keynote addresses to the world's leading financial service firms, Fortune 500 companies, universities, and national conferences. He is the founder and chairman of FinishRich Media, a company dedicated to revolutionizing the way people learn about money. Prior to founding FinishRich Media, he was a senior vice president of Morgan Stanley and a partner of The Bach Group, which during his tenure (1993 to 2001) managed more than half a billion dollars for individual investors.

As part of his mission, David Bach is involved with many worthwhile causes, including serving on the board of Habitat for Humanity New York.

David Bach lives in New York with his family. Please visit his website at www.finishrich.com.

The bestselling series by
DAVID BACH

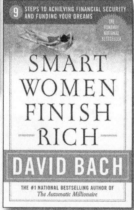

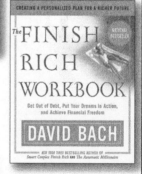

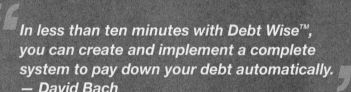